100-Day PANTRY

QUICK AND EASY GOURMET MEALS

100-Day PANTRY

QUICK AND EASY GOURMET MEALS

JAN JACKSON

CFI
SPRINGVILLE, UTAH

ISBN 13: 978-0-88290-969-1

Published by CFI, an imprint of Cedar Fort, Inc., 2373 W. 700 S., Springville, UT 84663
Distributed by Cedar Fort, Inc. www.cedarfort.com

LIBRARY OF CONGRESS CATALOGING-IN-PUBLICATION DATA
Jackson, Jan, 1945-
    100-day pantry : 100 quick and easy gourmet meals / Jan Jackson.
      p. cm.
    Includes index.
    ISBN 978-0-88290-969-1
1. Quick and easy cookery. 2. Food--Storage. I. Title. II. Title:
Hundred day pantry. III. Title: One hundred day pantry.

    TX833.5.J33 2010
    641.5--dc22

2010004652

Cover design by Megan Whittier
Cover design © 2010 by Lyle Mortimer
Edited and typeset by Megan E. Welton
Author Photo by Marie Wilkes

Printed in the United States of America
10   9   8   7   6   5

Printed on acid-free paper

For Steve.
People tell me you would be so proud.

Contents

Veggies

Beef

Fish

Acknowledgments

Thank you to friends and family who were enthusiastic and encouraging about the need for recipes of this type. You kept asking for my recipes until I finally decided there ought to be a book. Special thanks to my daughter-in-law Tisha, who joined me, tasting spoon in hand, to try many a recipe.

Introduction

The purpose of this book is to help you prepare your pantry so that you can eat from it for one hundred days. The recipes are designed so that all the makings can be stored for at least two years. No "outside" ingredients are needed—nothing fresh or frozen, and no water. By using broth as liquid when preparing noodles or rice, you can save your precious water storage for drinking.

When people begin to feel threatened or insecure, we stock up on canned goods. We go buy stuff we use a lot, like tuna and peaches. But we often don't really have a plan for turning those cans into tasty, appealing meals. These recipes solve that problem and let you stock your pantry so that it will be useful, whether there is ever a calamity or not. In case of a disaster—general or personal—you will be able to feed your family one entrée per day. No one will starve. Servings are generous and based on the idea that it might be your only meal of the day. Some of the recipes serve four, some serve ten. You can figure out which ones will work best for your family.

You can fix these meals in a crock pot or casserole dish, in the microwave, in an electric skillet, in a pan on the stove, or in a Dutch oven over a fire. Some have the consistency of soup or stew; others are more like a casserole.

The ingredients used are ordinary things you can find at most grocery stores and probably already use in your regular cooking. You will need to be creative to figure out how to store and rotate everything. You might need to make some sacrifices. We tend to have so much stuff! But think about it. Doesn't it make sense to find room for things that will help keep your loved ones alive?

Rotation is really pretty simple. If you include one of these meals in your cooking just once a week, you will rotate everything in two years, with the extra benefit that your family will get accustomed to them. When you buy your supplies, use a laundry pen to mark the "use by" dates (if I can't find a "use by" date, I write the purchase date with a dollar sign in front of it). Anything that is about to hit its date can be used right away or donated to your local food bank and replaced with a new item. Eating these meals once a week will not be a hardship. If you are like me, you are accustomed to using fresh or frozen veggies and the thought of meals from cans is not all that appealing. But I promise you these dishes taste great. They are yummy. Most of them are low in fat and certainly better for you than the pizza you might order when you're in a time crunch. They also cost a lot less than that pizza, and you can get dinner fixed faster than the pizza delivery guy can get to your door.

Choose the night of the week that is the most hectic for your family and designate it as Pantry Night. There is nothing tricky or time consuming about getting these meals on the table. Most can be prepared on the stove top in less than twenty minutes. Because everything is already cooked, you only need to heat things through (or until the grain or pasta is tender). You can have the kids dump things in the crock pot after school, and it will be ready by the time the family gathers.

Can sizes do not have to be exact. Manufacturers make changes from time to time, and different brands may vary. The sizes given are guidelines. In soups and stews, a little more or less of this or that won't matter much.

Meats

For beef or chicken use a 12-ounce or 15-ounce can of chicken or roast beef. Use turkey if you'd rather. You can also use whole chicken in a can. If you have access to canned ground beef, it will work great too. Cans of ground beef are larger, so if you double the recipe, you don't have to use two cans. For the ham, you can use a one-pound canned ham (these are harder to find—sometimes they are available at Walgreen's), a can of Spam, or two smaller, tuna-sized cans of smoked ham (available at most major grocers and very good). If using Spam, dice it, brown it, and drain off the fat first. For fish, use the flat cans (about 5–6 ounces). You can use the larger cans of salmon if you prefer. If you like a lot of meat, you may decide to use two cans in some of the beef recipes. These recipes are intentionally designed to be light on meat.

Vegetables and Beans

Use the regular size cans (about 15 ounces), unless the recipe says otherwise. For mushrooms, tomato paste, and so on, assume the recipe calls for the usual, smaller cans.

Broths and Soups

Use the 14-ounce cans of broth and 10-ounce cans of soup. Use light, fat-free, or low sodium, whatever you prefer. The recipes include enough broth to cook any included grain or pasta and allow for the use of dried vegetables. Storing all that broth does take a lot of space, so you can substitute 2 bouillon cubes and 1¾ cups water for each can of broth, if conserving water isn't an issue. You should store enough broth to get you through two or three weeks of cooking, in case your calamity includes loss of fresh water. Most recipes with noodles will have a better texture if the noodles are cooked and drained separately, using plain water.

Cheese, Salad Dressings, and Condiments

These are used to approximate the flavors of the original recipe. I have specified the smallest sizes I could find on the shelves, assuming that you might not be able to refrigerate leftovers. Ketchup and barbecue sauce are hard to get in small sizes, so if you don't have refrigeration, plan to use the remainder of these and similar ingredients in another recipe within a day or two.

Dried Ingredients

The dried ingredients are the only components that you will probably not find on your local grocery store shelves. These are designed for long-term storage and will need to be purchased from a preparedness dealer. Because these dried foods are intended for long-term (five to ten years) storage, it might be smart to use fresh ingredients when you can and leave your #10 cans unopened. "Everyday" instructions are included for each recipe that includes dried ingredients. On the other hand, these dried ingredients make the preparation very simple and are sometimes less expensive. When you test out a recipe, you can use the "everyday" instructions, and then purchase the dried ingredients when you know which ones you want.

Rice and Dry Beans

Some recipes call for quick-cooking rice. If not otherwise specified, assume you can use regular rice. If your heating sources are limited, use quick-cooking rice. The recipes do not indicate whether to use white or brown rice. I prefer brown rice, but it will not store as long as white. If you use a lot of rice anyway, use whatever kind you like, and keep a quantity of white on hand that has been properly packaged for long-term quality. These recipes only call for canned beans, but you can certainly store and cook dry beans if you prefer.

Seasonings

The average kitchen will have most of the seasonings called for in these recipes. When you have decided which recipes to use, check your spice collection to be sure you have enough on hand to match the quantities you will need. Seasoning packets (taco, chili, and so on) are generally dated to be used within eighteen months. Some of the recipes call for seasoning packets, and you might want to add them here and there. Just be aware that they might not last the whole two years at high quality. Things like soy sauce and Worcestershire sauce do not have to be refrigerated, but it might be wise to store two or three smaller bottles, rather than one large one, to protect the quality.

Special Items

I've included a few "exotic" recipes. You might want to store just enough ingredients to make these once or twice. Something a little different helps raise spirits. Some of the recipes call for a more expensive item, like pearl onions or artichokes. Do what fits your family's taste buds and budget. My family loves olives, so I always have several dozen cans on hand. I figure if things are desperate, these "treat" items will help make everyone feel a bit better.

Juice and granola bars for breakfast would be great, if you can use them up before they go bad. A few cases of canned fruit would make nice accompaniments. Make sure you have plenty of daily vitamins for everyone. If you have traditional food storage items, like wheat and powdered eggs and such, you can use those for pancakes and breads and hot cereal.

Why bother?

Why are we doing this? What kind of calamity are we preparing for? Recent natural disasters around the world have proven that life is unpredictable. You might suddenly be cut off from your well-stocked grocery store (or it might be stripped bare in a panic). You might lose power. The water supply might become unsafe. Labor disputes or disease outbreaks might disrupt food distribution. For example, in the first few months of 2009, peanut butter disappeared from store shelves because it was tainted, and we had a flu pandemic scare. Civil unrest could make it unsafe to leave your house (we sure hope this won't happen in the United States, but I have a friend in another country who experienced this, also in 2009). Having food on hand will help you cope with such problems and can also cushion you in economic difficulties. It is empowering to know that you are prepared to weather a storm. A friend told me a story about her fourteen-year-old son's response when her family used a small windfall of money to stock up the pantry. When all the food was put away, her son said, "It gives me a feeling of peace to be in this room."

Peace of mind comes from feeling you have done all you can to prepare. When speaking with a financial planner, I asked: "If I have a little extra money, should I save? Should I spend it now on things I want before inflation makes it worth a lot less? Should I buy gold? Should I buy things to stay alive in a crisis?" The answer was insightful. "If things get so bad that people are trading a $500 gold coin for a loaf of bread, you'd be better off to have the bread."

The economic recession has caused people to reexamine their priorities and think more about how to secure the necessities of life. What could be a better investment than food? This is especially true when it is food you will actually use instead of storing it in a corner of the basement to be ignored. Think of all the money you spend on insurance, hoping that you will never really need it. Tell yourself that your stored food is edible insurance.

Will we really need three months' worth of food on hand? We can hope we will never experience a calamity. But, should the need arise, the more you have, the more you can share with your neighbors. The rule of thumb is, "Hope for the best and prepare for the worst." You have nothing to lose. You are going to use the food anyway.

Get your 72-hour kits. Store water. Store wheat, beans, rice, honey, salt, and so on. Have options for being without power.

Be a good scout—BE PREPARED

Bonus

These are great recipes for when the kids need to cook, especially because they require zero chopping or frying. These recipes are also handy for those days when you just don't want to think too hard about the old "What's for dinner?" question. When your schedule gets whammed, you know you can trust your pantry to make it quick and easy to get a good meal on the table, with no worries about needing to run to the store to find a missing ingredient. If you want to take dinner to a sick neighbor, you can do it without making an extra trip to the store.

As I put the recipes through the testing process, I was pleasantly surprised at how inexpensive they are. They are also tasty—not just things you would only eat to survive. My recipe testers were enthusiastic about how good the dishes were. If my testers gave a bad report, I took the recipe out of the book.

To use this book, I suggest you go get everything you need to make one dish. Try it out with your family. If they all like it, go buy enough to make it three times, and then get the ingredients for the next trial. Start small. Work toward a two-week supply and build from there as your budget allows. You might want to choose eight meals to do twelve times each or ten meals to do ten times each, or thirty meals to do three times each—whatever seems right for your family. In just a few weeks or months, you can enjoy the peace of mind of your own 100-day security pantry.

P.S. Don't forget to get a couple of good CAN OPENERS!

Chicken

African Chicken

Cans/Jars:
2 (14-oz.) cans chicken broth
½ cup extra crunchy peanut butter
1 (10- or 15-oz.) can chicken, undrained

Dried:
¼ cup dried celery
1 cup dried onion
½ cup dried bell pepper

Grain/Pasta:
1 cup quick-cooking rice

Seasonings:
1 dash hot pepper sauce, optional

Directions:

Pour 1 can of broth in a large pot and mix with peanut butter. Add all remaining ingredients, except rice, and bring to a boil. Stir in rice, turn heat to low, and let sit ten minutes or until rice is done, stirring once.

FOR EVERYDAY MEALS: Replace dried vegetables with 3 ribs celery, 2 onions, 1 red pepper, 1 green pepper, all thinly sliced. Omit 1 can broth. Cook rice separately, in water, then add at the end, or serve chicken mixture over rice.

Asian Chicken Soup

SERVES 6

Cans/Jars:

1 (10- to 15-oz.) can chicken
1 (15-oz.) can carrots
1 (15-oz.) can bean sprouts
1 (6-oz.) can mushrooms
1 (14-oz.) can chicken broth

Grain/Pasta:

2 oz. fine noodles (3 oz. Ramen* noodles are okay)

Seasonings:

1 Tbsp. onion flakes
1 tsp. garlic flakes
½ tsp. ginger
3–4 Tbsp. soy sauce
1 scant ½ tsp. apple cider vinegar

Directions:

Do not drain the vegetables. Combine all ingredients and simmer until noodles are soft.

*Ramen noodles are not labeled for two years' storage, so rotate them more often.

BBQ Chicken with Fruit

SERVES 6

Grain/Pasta:
1¼ cups rice

Cans/Jars:
1 (14-oz.) can chicken broth
1 (10- to 15-oz.) can chicken
1 (15-oz.) can pineapple tidbits
1 (11-oz.) can mandarin oranges
1 (16-oz.) bottle barbecue sauce

Dried:
¼ cup dried bell pepper
¼ cup dried onion

Directions:

Cook rice in broth in separate pan. Combine remaining ingredients—do not drain—and heat through. Serve over rice.

FOR EVERYDAY MEALS: Replace dried vegetables with double the amount of fresh. Drain the fruit.

Brunswick Stew

SERVES 6

Cans/Jars:

1 (10- to 15-oz.) can chicken
1 (15-oz.) can potatoes
1 (10-oz.) can tomato soup
1 (15-oz.) can stewed tomatoes
1 (15-oz.) can corn
1 (15-oz.) can lima beans

Seasonings:

3 Tbsp. onion flakes
1 bay leaf
½ tsp. Worcestershire sauce
salt & pepper

Directions:

Do not drain any ingredients. Combine all and heat through. Remove bay leaf before serving.

Buffalo Wing Chicken Soup

SERVES 4

Cans/Jars:
1 (10- to 15-oz.) can chicken
1 (15-oz.) can diced carrots
1 (15-oz.) can diced tomatoes
1 (14-oz.) can chicken broth
½ cup barbecue sauce

Dried:
½ cup dried onion
½ cup dried celery

Seasonings:
1 Tbsp. brown sugar
5-6 drops hot pepper sauce

Directions:

Do not drain any ingredients. Combine all and heat through.

FOR EVERYDAY MEALS: Replace dried vegetables with double the amount of fresh.

Cashew Chicken

SERVES 6

Cans/Jars:
1 (10- to 15-oz.) can chicken, with juices
1 (14-oz.) can chicken broth
1 (6-oz.) can mushrooms, undrained
1 (10-oz.) can cream of mushroom soup
1 (8-oz.) pkg. cashew pieces*

Grain/Pasta:
1 cup rice

Dried:
½ cup dried celery

Seasonings:
1 Tbsp. soy sauce

Directions:

Combine all except rice and nuts. Bring to a boil. Add rice and reduce heat to low for 10 minutes or until rice is done. Stir in nuts just before serving.

FOR EVERYDAY MEALS: Replace dried celery with one cup fresh.

*Nuts need to be kept in the fridge or freezer for long-term storage.

Cheesy Chicken & Beans

SERVES 6

Grain/Pasta:
6 oz. noodles

Dried:
¼ cup dried onion

Cans/Jars:
1 (14-oz.) can chicken broth
1 (10- to 15-oz.) can chicken, drained
1 (10-oz.) can chicken gravy
1 (15-oz.) can green beans, drained
1 (2-oz.) jar pimiento, drained, optional
1 (8-oz.) jar processed cheese

Seasonings:
1 tsp parsley flakes
¼ tsp. pepper

Directions:

Simmer noodles in broth until tender. Drain, leaving a little moist. Stir dried onions into noodles to absorb liquid. Add remaining ingredients. Heat through.

FOR EVERYDAY MEALS: Omit broth. Cook noodles in water. Replace dried onions with ½ cup fresh.

Cheesy Menudo

SERVES 6

Cans/Jars:
1 (10- to 15-oz.) can chicken
2 (15-oz.) cans hominy
1 (4-oz.) can diced green chilies
1 (8-oz.) block processed cheese, cubed

Seasonings:
1 tsp. garlic salt
½ tsp. pepper
1 Tbsp. dried parsley or cilantro

Directions:

Do not drain cans. Combine all but cheese and heat through. Stir in cheese and continue heating until cheese melts in.

Chicken a la King

Grain/Pasta:
1¼ cups rice

Cans/Jars:
1 (14-oz.) can chicken broth
1 (6-oz.) can mushrooms
1 (10- to 15-oz.) can chicken
2 (10-oz.) cans cream of chicken soup
1 (2-oz.) jar pimiento, drained

Dried:
½ cup sour cream powder
¼ cup dried onion
¼ cup dried celery
¼ cup dried bell pepper

Directions:

Cook rice in broth in a separate pan. Drain juice from mushrooms and chicken into pot. Whisk in sour cream powder, then add dried vegetables. Add remaining ingredients and stir to combine. Simmer for about 10 minutes. Serve over rice.

FOR EVERYDAY MEALS: Replace dried vegetables with double the amount of fresh. Sauté vegetables in a bit of olive oil before combining with other ingredients. Omit broth and cook rice in water. Drain chicken and mushrooms. Replace sour cream powder with ½ cup fresh and add at the end.

Chicken Artichoke Curry

SERVES 6

Grain/Pasta:
1 cup couscous

Cans/Jars:
1 (14-oz.) can chicken broth
1 (6-oz.) can mushrooms
1 (5-oz.) can sliced water chestnuts
2 (10- to 15-oz.) cans chicken
1 (15-oz.) can artichoke hearts, quartered & drained
1 (10-oz.) can cream of mushroom soup

Dried:
1 cup sour cream powder

Seasonings:
1 tsp. curry powder
1 tsp. lemon juice (or ½ tsp. cider vinegar)

Directions:

Cook couscous in broth according to the directions on the couscous package. Drain juice from mushrooms and water chestnuts into pot. Whisk in sour cream powder until dissolved. Add all other ingredients and heat through. Serve over couscous.

OR: Pour broth in crock pot and whisk in sour cream powder; add all remaining ingredients, except lemon juice. Heat on low 2 hours. add lemon juice just before serving.

FOR EVERYDAY MEALS: Replace sour cream powder with 1 cup fresh sour cream. Omit lemon juice/vinegar. Do not use juices from mushrooms and water chestnuts. Add ¼ cup mayonnaise. Top with chopped pecans or slivered almonds.

Chicken Azteca

Cans/Jars:

1 (14-oz.) can chicken broth
2 (10- to 15-oz.) cans chicken, undrained
2 (15-oz.) cans black beans, rinsed & drained
2 (15-oz.) cans corn, drained
1 (16-oz.) jar salsa
1 (15-oz.) jar Mexican-style cheese (queso)*

Grain/Pasta

1 cup rice

Dried:

1 cup sour cream powder

Seasonings:

1 tsp. cumin

Directions:

Pour broth into pot. Whisk in sour cream powder until dissolved. Add all other ingredients and cook until rice is done, stirring occasionally.

For EVERYDAY MEALS: Replace sour cream powder with 1 cup fresh sour cream and wait until end of cooking to add it.

*Queso can be spicy. Buy the mild or hot, or use just half the jar, according to your family's taste.

Chicken & Beef Pot Luck

SERVES 10

Cans/Jars:
1 (10- to 15-oz.) can beef
1 (10- to 15-oz.) can chicken
2 (15-oz.) cans diced potatoes
1 (15-oz.) can carrots
1 (15-oz.) can lima beans
1 (15-oz.) can corn
1 (15-oz.) can diced tomatoes

Dried:
1 cup dried onion
½ cup dried bell pepper
½ cup dried celery
½ cup dried broccoli

Seasonings:
1 tsp. mustard powder
½ tsp. chili powder
¼ cup dried parsley
salt & pepper

Directions:

Drain juices from cans into pot and stir in dried vegetables, allowing them to absorb the moisture for 2 or 3 minutes. Add remaining ingredients and heat through.

FOR EVERYDAY MEALS: Replace dried vegetables with double the amount of fresh. Drain potatoes, carrots, and limas.

Chicken Barley Soup

Cans/Jars:

1 (10- to 15-oz.) can chicken, undrained
2 oz. bacon crumbles
1 (15-oz.) can green beans, undrained
1 (12-oz.) can V-8 juice
1 (14-oz.) can chicken broth

Grain/Pasta:

½ cup barley

Directions:

Combine all and simmer until barley is done, stirring occasionally. The barley will take about 45 or 50 minutes on the stovetop or 3–4 hours in a crock pot.

Chicken Basil

SERVES 6

Grain/Pasta:
6 oz. pasta

Cans/Jars:
1 (14-oz.) can chicken broth
1 (10- to 15-oz.) can chicken, undrained
1 (15-oz.) can carrots, drained
1 (6-oz.) can mushrooms, undrained, optional
1 (15- to 20-oz.) jar Alfredo sauce

Dried:
½ cup dried broccoli

Seasonings:
1 Tbsp. basil
salt & pepper

Directions:

Simmer pasta in broth until softened, stirring occasionally. Add remaining ingredients and heat through.

FOR EVERYDAY MEALS: Replace dried broccoli with 1 cup fresh or frozen. Cook and drain pasta separately; add at the end, after the broccoli is tender.

Chicken Biddy Soup

Grain/Pasta:
6 oz. fettuccini

Cans/Jars:
1 (14-oz.) can chicken broth
1 (10- to 15-oz.) can chicken
1 (8-oz.) can tomato sauce
1 (10-oz.) can chicken vegetable soup
1 (15-oz.) can potatoes
1 (15-oz.) can carrots
1 (10-oz.) can cheddar cheese soup

Dried:
½ cup dried onion
½ cup dried bell pepper

Seasoning:
1 tsp. garlic flakes
1 Tbsp. herb seasoning
salt & pepper

Directions:

Simmer noodles in broth in large pot until softened. Do not drain vegetables. Add all ingredients and heat through.

FOR EVERYDAY MEALS: Omit broth and cook noodles in water. Replace dried vegetables with double the amount of fresh.

Chicken Broccoli Alfredo

SERVES 4-6

Cans/Jars:
1 (10- to 15-oz.) can chicken
1 (24- to 30-oz.) jar Alfredo sauce
1 (14-oz.) can chicken broth
1 (6-oz.) can mushrooms

Grain/Pasta:
8 oz. linguine

Dried:
½ cup dried broccoli

Seasonings:
salt & pepper

Directions:

Mix all ingredients together and simmer until linguine is done, stirring occasionally. Continue to heat on low until liquid has reduced to the texture you like.

FOR EVERYDAY MEALS: Replace dried broccoli with 1 cup fresh or frozen. Omit broth. Cook linguine separately and serve chicken mixture on top of pasta.

Chicken Capri

Cans/Jars:

1 (10- to 15-oz.) can chicken, undrained
1 (15-oz.) can diced tomatoes
1 (6-oz.) can tomato juice
1 (6-oz.) can mushrooms, undrained, optional
1 (14-oz.) can chicken broth

Grain/Pasta:

1 cup couscous

Dried:

½ cup dried bell pepper
½ cup dried onion

Seasonings:

1 Tbsp. garlic flakes
½ tsp. rosemary
salt & pepper

Directions:

Cook couscous in broth according to the directions on the couscous package. Combine remaining ingredients and heat through. Serve over couscous.

FOR EVERYDAY MEALS: Replace dried vegetables with double the amount of fresh. Omit tomato juice.

Chicken Caravan

SERVES 6

Grain/Pasta:
1 cup couscous

Cans/Jars:
1 (14-oz.) can chicken broth
1 (10- to 15-oz.) can chicken
1 (15-oz.) can carrots
1 (15-oz.) can diced potatoes
2 (15-oz.) cans zucchini with tomatoes
1 (15-oz.) can garbanzo beans

Dried:
½ cup dried onion
½ cup raisins

Seasonings:
2 Tbsp. garlic flakes
1 tsp. ginger
½ tsp. cumin
¼ tsp. cinnamon
2 Tbsp. dried parsley
salt & pepper
½ tsp. turmeric, optional
¼ tsp. cayenne, optional

Directions:

Cook couscous in broth in separate pan according to the directions on the couscous package. Simmer remaining ingredients in a pot until onions are tender. Serve over couscous.

FOR EVERYDAY MEALS: Replace dried onion with 1 cup fresh, sliced. Drain carrots, potatoes, and garbanzo beans.

Chicken Chow Mein

Cans/Jars:
1 (10- to 15-oz.) can chicken
1 (6-oz.) can mushrooms
1 (14-oz.) can bean sprouts
1 (5-oz.) can bamboo shoots

Grain/Pasta:
1 (5-oz.) can chow mein noodles*

Dried:
1 cup dried onion
½ cup dried celery

Seasonings:
2 Tbsp. soy sauce
1 tsp. sugar
¼ tsp. ginger

Directions:

Do not drain cans. Combine all but chow mein noodles. Heat through. Serve over noodles.

FOR EVERYDAY MEALS: Replace dried vegetables with twice the amount of fresh, cut in chunks. Drain the cans, except the chicken.

*Chow mein noodles are not labeled for 2 years' storage, so rotate them more often.

Chicken Corn Chowder

SERVES 8

Cans/Jars:
1 (10- to 15-oz.) can chicken
1 (15-oz.) can potatoes, undrained
1 (14-oz.) can chicken broth
2 (12-oz.) cans evaporated milk
2 (15-oz.) cans creamed corn
1 (15-oz.) can corn, undrained
1 (2-oz.) jar pimiento, drained, optional

Dried:
½ cup dried onion
½ cup dried celery

Seasonings:
1 tsp. parsley flakes
salt & pepper

Directions:
Combine all ingredients and heat through.

FOR EVERYDAY MEALS: Replace dried vegetables with double the amount of fresh. Drain potatoes.

Chicken Creole

Grain/Pasta:
1¼ cups rice

Cans/Jars:
1 (14-oz.) can chicken broth
1 (10- to 15-oz.) can chicken
1 (5-oz.) can ham
1 (15-oz.) can diced tomatoes
1 (6-oz.) can tomato paste

Dried:
½ cup dried bell pepper
¼ cup dried onion

Seasonings:
salt & pepper
Several drops hot pepper sauce

Directions:

Cook rice in broth in a separate pan. Combine remaining ingredients and heat through. Stir in rice.

FOR EVERYDAY MEALS: Replace dried vegetables with double the amount of fresh.

Chicken Fettuccine

SERVES 4

Cans/Jars:
2 (14-oz.) cans chicken broth
1 (10- to 15-oz.) can chicken, undrained
1 (15-oz.) can mixed vegetables, drained
8 oz. jar Parmesan cheese

Dried:
1 cup sour cream powder
1 cup powdered milk

Grain/Pasta:
8 oz. fettuccini

Seasonings:
1 Tbsp. garlic flakes
1 Tbsp. parsley flakes
salt & pepper

Directions:

In a large pot, combine ½ cup broth and juice from chicken. Whisk in powdered milk and powdered sour cream. In another pot, simmer fettuccine in remaining broth until done, stirring occasionally. Drain, reserving broth. Meanwhile, add remaining ingredients to sour cream mixture and heat until cheese melts, stirring occasionally. If mixture is too thick, add in additional broth. Serve over noodles. If desired, reserve some Parmesan to use as a garnish. If you have leftovers, stir in any remaining broth before storing; recipe gets stiffer as it sits.

FOR EVERYDAY MEALS: Replace powdered milk with 1½ cups fresh; replace sour cream powder with 1 cup fresh. Omit broth and cook fettuccine in water.

Chicken Macaroni Stew

SERVES 6

Cans/Jars:
1 (10- to 15-oz.) can chicken
2 (6-oz.) cans mushrooms
1 (15-oz.) can carrots
1 (15-oz.) can green beans
1 (15-oz.) can diced tomatoes
1 (14-oz.) can chicken broth

Dried:
¼ cup dried onion

Seasonings:
2 tsp. Italian seasoning
salt & pepper

Grain/Pasta:
1 cup macaroni

Directions:

Do not drain any cans; use all the juices. Mix all ingredients together except macaroni. Bring mixture to a boil, add macaroni and simmer, covered, until macaroni is tender.

For EVERYDAY MEALS: Replace dried onion with ½ cup fresh.

Chicken Mushroom Stew

SERVES 4-6

Cans/Jars:

1 (10- to 15-oz.) can chicken, undrained
1 (6-oz.) can mushrooms, undrained
1 (15-oz.) can zucchini with tomatoes
1 (6-oz.) can tomato paste
1 (14-oz.) can chicken broth

Dried:

½ cup dried onion
⅓ cup dried bell pepper

Seasonings:

2 Tbsp. garlic flakes
1 Tbsp. Italian seasoning

Directions:

Combine all ingredients and heat through.

For EVERYDAY MEALS: Replace dried vegetables with double the amount of fresh.

Chicken Noodle Soup, Traditional

Cans/Jars:

1 (10- to 15-oz.) can chicken

3 (14-oz.) cans chicken broth

2 (15-oz.) cans carrots & peas, undrained

Grain/Pasta:

6 oz. noodles

Dried:

¼ cup dried celery

¼ cup dried onion

Seasonings:

1 tsp. basil

1 Tbsp. butter powder

salt & pepper

Directions:

Combine all and simmer until noodles are done, stirring occasionally.

FOR EVERYDAY MEALS: Replace dried vegetables with double the amount of fresh.

Chicken Noodle Soup with Bacon

SERVES 6

Cans/Jars:

1 (10- to 15-oz.) can chicken
1 (15-oz.) can corn
1 (15-oz.) can peas
1 (15-oz.) can green beans
2 (14-oz.) cans chicken broth
1 oz. bacon crumbles

Grain/Pasta:

6-oz. noodles

Directions:

Do not drain cans; use all the juices. Combine all ingredients and simmer until noodles are done, stirring occasionally.

Chicken Paprika

Cans/Jars:
1 (10- to 15-oz.) can chicken
1 (6-oz.) can mushrooms
1 (12-oz.) can evaporated milk
1 (14-oz.) can chicken broth

Grain/Pasta:
6 oz. noodles

Dried:
½ cup dried onion
¼ cup dried celery
1 cup sour cream powder

Seasonings:
2 tsp. paprika, divided
2 tsp. garlic flakes
salt & pepper

Directions:

Simmer noodles in broth until softened. Drain juice from chicken into a bowl and whisk in sour cream powder and 1 tsp. paprika. Set aside. Combine remaining ingredients. Add undrained noodles and bring to a simmer. Add sour cream mixture and heat through.

FOR EVERYDAY MEALS: Replace dried vegetables with double the amount of fresh. Replace sour cream powder with 1 cup fresh. Omit broth and cook noodles separately.

Chicken Rice Stew

SERVES 6

Cans/Jars:
1 (10- to 15-oz.) can chicken, undrained
1 (10-oz.) can cream of mushroom soup
1 (6-oz.) can mushrooms, undrained
1 (15-oz.) can carrots, undrained
1 (14-oz.) can chicken broth

Grain/Pasta:
1 cup rice

Seasonings:
2 tsp. celery flakes
½ tsp. garlic powder
salt & pepper

Directions:

Combine all and simmer until rice is done, stirring occasionally.

Chicken Taco Rice

SERVES 4-6

Cans/Jars:
1 (10- to 15-oz.) can chicken, undrained
1 (14-oz.) can chicken broth
1 (8-oz.) can tomato sauce
1 (15-oz.) can corn, undrained
1 (8-oz.) jar processed cheese

Seasonings:
1 Tbsp. taco seasoning
salt & pepper

Grain/Pasta:
1½ cups quick-cooking rice

Directions:

Mix all ingredients except rice and cheese. Bring to a boil. Stir in rice, cover, and reduce heat to low. Cook 10 minutes or until rice is done. Stir in cheese.

Chicken Taco Soup

SERVES 4

Cans/Jars:
1 (10- to 15-oz.) can chicken
1 (15-oz.) can corn
1 (16-oz.) jar salsa
1 (14-oz.) can chicken broth
1 (15-oz.) can ranch beans, optional
1 (4-oz.) can green chilies, optional

Grain/Pasta:
½ cup rice, regular or quick cooking

Directions:
Do not drain cans; use all the juices. Mix all ingredients together and simmer until rice is done.

Chicken Tetrazzini

Grain/Pasta:
8 oz. spaghetti, broken

Cans/Jars:
1 (14-oz.) can chicken broth
1 (10- to 15-oz.) can chicken, undrained
1 (10-oz.) can cream of chicken soup
1 (6-oz.) can mushrooms, undrained
1 (12-oz.) can evaporated milk
1 (8-oz.) jar processed cheese
½ cup Parmesan cheese

Seasonings:
1 Tbsp. onion flakes
¼ tsp. marjoram
3-4 drops hot pepper sauce, optional

Directions:

Simmer spaghetti in broth in large pot, until softened. Add remaining ingredients except Parmesan cheese. Simmer for about 10 minutes, stirring occasionally. Top each serving with Parmesan.

Chicken Veggie Bake

SERVES 6

Cans/Jars:

1 (10- to 15-oz.) can chicken, drained
2 (15-oz.) cans sliced potatoes, drained
1 (15-oz.) can green beans, drained
1 (5-oz.) can water chestnuts, drained
1 (8-oz.) bottle Italian dressing
¼ cup Parmesan cheese

Seasonings:

1 tsp. garlic powder

Directions:

Mix chicken and dressing in 8x8 casserole dish. Add other ingredients and stir gently. Top with cheese. Bake at 400° for 20–25 minutes.

Four-bean Chicken Chili

SERVES 8

Cans/Jars:

1 (15-oz.) can black beans, rinsed & drained
1 (10- to 15-oz.) can chicken
1 (15-oz.) can pinto beans
1 (15-oz.) can white beans
1 (15-oz.) can kidney beans
2 (15-oz.) cans Mexican-style tomatoes
1 (11-oz.) can Mexican-style corn

Dried:

½ cup dried onion

Seasonings:

1 tsp. garlic flakes
1 tsp cumin
4-6 drops hot pepper sauce, optional
1 bay leaf

Directions:

Do not drain any cans except the black beans. Mix all ingredients together and heat through. Remove bay leaf before serving.

FOR EVERYDAY MEALS: Replace dried onion with 1 cup fresh.

Italian Chicken

SERVES 4-6

Grain/Pasta:
6 oz. pasta

Cans/Jars:
1 (14-oz.) can chicken broth
1 (10- to 15-oz.) can chicken, drained
1 (6-oz.) can mushrooms, drained
2 (15-oz.) cans Italian-style tomatoes
½ cup Parmesan cheese

Seasonings:
1 tsp. Italian seasoning
1 tsp. garlic flakes
1 Tbsp. dried parsley

Directions:

Simmer pasta in broth until softened. Combine remaining ingredients except Parmesan and parsley. Bring to a simmer, stir in drained pasta and heat through. Garnish each serving with Parmesan and parsley.

Jambalaya

Grain/Pasta:
1¼ cup rice

Cans/Jars:
1 (14-oz.) can chicken broth
1 (10- to 15-oz.) can chicken
1 (4-oz.) can shrimp
1 (15-oz.) can carrots
1 (15-oz.) can diced tomatoes

Dried:
1 cup dried onion

Seasonings:
1 tsp. garlic flakes
½ tsp. basil
salt & pepper

Directions:

Cook rice in broth. In separate pot, drain juices from chicken, shrimp, and carrots. Stir dried onions into the juices and let sit for a few minutes to absorb moisture. Add remaining ingredients and heat through. Serve over rice.

OR: Combine all ingredients in crock pot and heat on low 3–4 hours.

FOR EVERYDAY MEALS: Drain carrots and chicken. Replace dried onions with 3 fresh onions, chopped. Sauté onions in a little oil before combining ingredients. Omit broth. Cook rice separately.

Mediterranean Chicken

SERVES 4

Grain/Pasta:
1¼ cup rice

Cans/Jars:
1 (14-oz.) can chicken broth
1 (6-oz.) jar marinated artichokes
1 (10- to 15-oz.) can chicken
1 (6-oz.) can mushroom pieces

Dried:
½ cup dried onion
½ cup dried spinach

Seasonings:
1 tsp. garlic flakes
2 Tbsp. red wine vinegar
salt & pepper

Directions:

Cook rice in broth. Drain juices from artichokes, chicken, and mushrooms into separate pot. Stir in dried vegetables and let sit for a couple of minutes to absorb moisture. Cut artichokes into smaller pieces (run a knife through the jar a few times). Add all other ingredients and heat through over low heat. Serve over rice.

FOR EVERYDAY MEALS: Replace dried onion and spinach with double the amount of fresh. Drain mushrooms. Sauté onions in artichoke juices for 3–4 minutes before adding other ingredients.

Mexican Chicken Casserole

Grain/Pasta:
6 oz. crinkly noodles

Cans/Jars:
1 (14-oz.) can chicken broth
1 (10- to 15-oz.) can chicken
1 (10-oz.) can cream of mushroom soup
1 (10-oz.) can cream of chicken soup
1 (15-oz.) can Mexican-style tomatoes (spicy if you like)
1 (2.5-oz.) can sliced olives, drained
1 (8-oz.) block processed cheese, cubed

Dried:
½ cup sour cream powder
½ cup dried onions
¼ cup dried bell pepper

Directions:

Simmer noodles in broth until softened. Drain juice from chicken into a separate pot and whisk in sour cream powder. Add the remaining ingredients except the cheese and noodles, and heat through. If mixture seems dry, add some liquid from noodles. Then stir in the cheese and drained noodles, and continue heating until the cheese melts in. (Or save half of the cheese, turn mixture into a casserole dish, arrange cheese on top and bake 15–20 minutes at 350°.)

FOR EVERYDAY MEALS: Replace dried vegetables with double the amount of fresh. Replace sour cream with ½ cup fresh. Omit broth. Cook and drain noodles before adding to other ingredients.

Mulligan Stew

SERVES 6

Cans/Jars:
1 (10- to 15-oz.) can chicken
2 oz. bacon crumbles
2 (15-oz.) cans diced tomatoes
1 (15-oz.) can corn
1 (15-oz.) can diced potatoes
1 (15-oz.) can lima beans

Dried:
¼ cup dried onion

Seasonings:
salt & pepper
Dash of cayenne, optional

Directions:

Do not drain cans; use all the juices. Mix all ingredients together and heat through.

For EVERYDAY MEALS: Replace dried onion with ½ cup fresh.

Pumpkin Chili

Cans/Jars:
1 (10- to 15-oz.) can chicken, with juice
2 (15-oz.) cans black beans, rinsed and drained
1 (15-oz.) can pumpkin puree
1 (15-oz.) can diced tomatoes
1 (14-oz.) can chicken broth

Dried:
½ cup dried bell pepper
½ cup dried onion

Seasonings:
1½ tsp. oregano
2 tsp. cumin
2 tsp. chili powder

Directions:
Combine all ingredients and heat through.

FOR EVERYDAY MEALS: Replace dried vegetables with double the amount of fresh.

Quick Chicken

SERVES 4

Grain/Pasta:
1¼ cups rice

Cans/Jars:
1 (10- to 15-oz.) can chicken
2 (10-oz.) cans chicken gumbo soup
1 (14-oz.) can chicken broth

Directions:

Cook rice in broth in separate pan. Heat chicken and gumbo together. Serve over rice.

Scalloped Chicken & Corn

SERVES 6

Grain/Pasta:
6 oz. macaroni

Cans/Jars:
1 (14-oz.) can chicken broth
1 (10- to 15-oz.) can chicken
1 (15-oz.) can creamed corn
1 (10-oz.) can cream of chicken soup
1 (8-oz.) block processed cheese, cubed

Dried:
¼ cup dried onion
½ cup dried celery

Seasonings:
1 tsp. parsley flakes
⅛ tsp. pepper

Directions:

Simmer macaroni in broth until almost done. Drain off most of the broth. Stir dried vegetables into the macaroni and let sit for a moment to absorb the warm moisture. Combine with remaining ingredients and spread in greased 8x12 casserole dish. Bake at 375° for 25 minutes.

FOR EVERYDAY MEALS: Replace dried vegetables with double the amount of fresh. Omit broth. Cook macaroni in water.

Southern Chicken Curry

SERVES 4

Cans/Jars:
1 (14-oz.) can chicken broth
1 12- to (15-oz.) can chicken
1 (15-oz.) diced tomatoes
½ cup slivered almonds, for garnish*

Dried:
⅔ cup dried onion
¼ cup dried celery
½ cup dried bell pepper
½ cup raisins, for garnish

Grain/Pasta:
1 cup rice

Seasonings:
1 Tbsp. garlic flakes
1 Tbsp. curry powder
salt & pepper

Directions:

Pour ⅓ cup broth in pot and stir in dried vegetables. Cook rice in remaining broth. Add all other ingredients except raisins and almonds. Heat through and serve over rice. Top each serving with raisins and almonds.

FOR EVERYDAY MEALS: Omit broth and cook rice in water. Omit dried vegetables and replace with double the amount of fresh.

*Store nuts in fridge or freezer.

Sweet & Sour Chicken

SERVES 6-8

Grain/Pasta:
1¼ cups rice

Cans/Jars:
1 (14-oz.) can chicken broth
1 (10- to 15-oz.) can chicken
1 (15-oz.) can pineapple tidbits
1 (5-oz.) can water chestnuts
1 (6-oz.) can mushrooms
1 (10-oz.) jar sweet & sour sauce

Dried:
¼ cup dried onion
½ cup dried bell pepper
¼ cup dried celery

Seasonings:
1 Tbsp. soy sauce
1 Tbsp. brown sugar
2 tsp. vinegar

Directions:
Cook rice in broth. In a separate pan, combine remaining ingredients and heat through. Do not drain cans. Serve over rice.

FOR EVERYDAY MEALS: Omit broth and cook rice in water. Replace dried vegetables with double the amount of fresh. Drain water chestnuts and mushrooms.

Tamale Chicken

SERVES 4-6

Cans/Jars:

1 (2.5-oz.) can sliced olives
1 (4-oz.) can diced chilies
1 (10- to 15-oz.) can chicken
1 (10- to 15-oz.) can beef tamales, cut up
1 (10-oz.) can cream of chicken soup
1 (15-oz.) can diced tomatoes
1 (8-oz.) jar processed cheese

Dried:

1 cup sour cream powder
½ cup dried onion

Seasonings:

1 tsp. chili powder
1 tsp. pepper

Directions:

Drain olives and chilies into pot. Whisk in sour cream powder. Stir in all remaining ingredients and heat through.

FOR EVERYDAY MEALS: Replace dried onion with 1 cup fresh. Replace sour cream powder with 1 cup fresh. Drain olives and chilies.

Tex-Mex Chicken & Rice

SERVES 10-12

Cans/Jars:

2 (29-oz.) cans refried beans
1 (15-oz.) jar Mexican-style cheese (queso)*
1 (10- to 15-oz.) can chicken
2 (15-oz.) cans diced tomatoes
1 (6-oz.) can tomato paste
1 (4-oz.) can diced green chilies
2 (14-oz.) cans chicken broth

Dried:

1 cup dried onions
½ cup dried bell pepper

Seasonings:

3 tsp. garlic powder, divided
2 tsp. cumin
2 Tbsp. taco seasoning

Grain/Pasta:

1 cup rice

Directions:

Mix beans with 2 teaspoons garlic powder, 2 teaspoons cumin, and queso. Heat slowly, stirring occasionally. Bring all remaining ingredients except rice to boil in a separate pot. Stir in rice, cover, reduce heat, and simmer until rice is done. Serve with bean mixture.

FOR EVERYDAY MEALS: Omit 1 can broth. Replace dried vegetables with 2 fresh onions and 1 green pepper, chopped.

*Queso can be spicy. You might want to use just half the jar or replace with processed cheese or use the mildest queso.

White Bean Chicken Chili

SERVES 6

Cans/Jars:
1 (12-oz.) can evaporated milk
1 (10- to 15-oz.) can chicken, undrained
2 (15-oz.) cans great northern beans, undrained
1 (4-oz.) can diced green chilies, undrained
1 (10-oz.) can cream of chicken soup

Dried:
½ cup sour cream powder
½ cup dried green peppers
½ cup dried onions

Seasonings:
1 Tbsp. cumin
1 Tbsp. garlic flakes
1 tsp. oregano
2 Tbsp. dried cilantro

Directions:
Pour evaporated milk into pot. Whisk sour cream powder into milk until dissolved. Add all other ingredients and heat through, stirring occasionally.

FOR EVERYDAY MEALS: Replace dried onions and peppers with fresh, 1 cup of each. Drain beans. Replace dried sour cream with ½ cup fresh and add at the end.

Veggies

Basil Tomato Soup

Cans/Jars:

1 (10-oz.) can tomato soup
1 (15-oz.) can diced tomatoes
2 (14-oz.) cans vegetable broth
¼ cup Parmesan cheese

Grain/Pasta:

½ cup corkscrew pasta

Seasonings:

1½ tsp. basil
1 Tbsp. sugar

Directions:

Combine all ingredients except Parmesan. Simmer until pasta is done. Sprinkle Parmesan on each serving.

Black Bean Veggie Soup

SERVES 6

Cans/Jars:

2 (15-oz.) cans black beans, rinsed & drained
1 (15-oz.) can diced tomatoes
1 (15-oz.) can corn, undrained
1 (16-oz.) jar salsa
1 (14-oz.) can vegetable broth
1 (8-oz.) jar processed cheese

Dried:

¼ cup dried bell pepper

Seasonings:

2 tsp. cumin
2 Tbsp. garlic flakes

Directions:

Combine all ingredients except cheese. Bring to a simmer. Add cheese and stir gently until it melts in.

FOR EVERYDAY MEALS: Replace dried peppers with ½ cup fresh.

Broccoli Cheese Soup

Cans/Jars:

4 (10-oz.) cans cream of potato soup

4 (12-oz.) cans evaporated milk

1 (16-oz.) block processed cheese, cubed

Dried:

1 cup dried broccoli

Directions:

Combine all ingredients except cheese in pot. Simmer 10 minutes. Add cheese and stir until cheese melts.

FOR EVERYDAY MEALS: Replace dried broccoli with 1 lb. frozen, chopped.

Carrot Curry Soup

SERVES 4

Cans/Jars:
1 (14-oz.) can chicken broth
2 (15-oz.) cans carrots, undrained

Dried:
½ cup sour cream powder
½ cup dried onion

Seasonings:
1 Tbsp. sugar
1 tsp. ginger
1 tsp. curry powder
2 Tbsp. chives, for garnish

Directions:

Pour broth into pot. Whisk in sour cream powder until dissolved. Add other ingredients except chives. Heat through. Run a wand blender through the pot to partially puree. Garnish each serving with chives.

FOR EVERYDAY MEALS: Replace dried onion with 1 cup fresh. Replace sour cream with ½ cup fresh.

Italian Bean Soup

SERVES 8

Cans/Jars:

1 (15-oz.) can diced Italian-style tomatoes
1 (15-oz.) can great northcrn beans
1 (6-oz.) can mushrooms
1 (15-oz.) can green beans
1 (10-oz.) can tomato soup
1 (14-oz.) can vegetable broth
¼ cup Parmesan cheese

Dried:

¼ cup dried onion

Seasonings:

1 Tbsp. Italian seasoning
1 tsp. garlic flakes
1 tsp. sugar

Directions:

Do not drain cans; use all the juices. Combine all ingredients except Parmesan cheese and heat through. Sprinkle each serving with Parmesan cheese.

FOR EVERYDAY MEALS: Replace dried onion with ½ cup fresh.

Mexican Tomato Corn Soup

SERVES 8

Cans/Jars:
1 (15-oz.) can diced carrots, undrained
1 (15-oz.) can Italian-style tomatoes
2½ cups tomato juice
2 (14-oz.) cans chicken broth
2 (15-oz.) cans corn, undrained
1 (4-oz.) can diced green chilies, undrained

Dried:
½ cup dried onion
½ cup dried bell pepper

Seasonings:
1 tsp. garlic flakes
1 tsp. chili powder
1½ tsp. cumin
1 dash cayenne

Directions:
Combine all ingredients and heat through.

Variation:
Add beef or chicken; add kidney beans or 2 oz. noodles; substitute 1 tablespoon taco seasoning for the three spices.

FOR EVERYDAY MEALS: Replace dried vegetables with double the amount of fresh.

Minestrone

Cans/Jars:

1 (15-oz.) can diced tomatoes
1 (8-oz.) can tomato sauce
1 (15-oz.) can kidney beans
1 (15-oz.) can carrots
1 (14-oz.) can vegetable broth

Dried:

⅓ cup dried onions
⅓ cup dried celery
⅓ cup dried spinach

Seasonings:

1 tsp. garlic flakes
1 Tbsp. Italian seasoning
1 tsp. parsley flakes

Grain/Pasta:

½ cup macaroni

Directions:

Do not drain cans. Mix all ingredients together and simmer until macaroni is done, stirring occasionally.

FOR EVERYDAY MEALS: Replace dried vegetables with double the amount of fresh.

Pasta Grande

SERVES 4

Grain/Pasta:
1½ cups corkscrew pasta

Cans/Jars:
2 (14-oz.) cans vegetable broth
1 (15-oz.) can diced tomatoes
1 (15-oz.) can kidney beans

Dried:
½ cup sour cream powder
¼ cup dried onion
¼ cup dried bell pepper

Seasonings:
2 tsp. chili seasoning
1 Tbsp. parsley flakes
1 Tbsp. brown sugar

Directions:

Simmer pasta in broth until softened. Drain liquid from pasta into pot and whisk in sour cream powder, stirring until powder is dissolved. Combine all ingredients and heat through.

FOR EVERYDAY MEALS: Replace dried vegetables with double the amount of fresh. Replace sour cream powder with ½ cup fresh. Omit broth. Cook pasta in water and drain before combining all ingredients.

Pizza Beans

Cans/Jars:

2 (15-oz.) cans pinto beans, undrained
1 (15-oz.) can garbanzo beans, undrained
1 (15-oz.) can diced tomatoes
8-oz. grated Parmesan cheese

Dried:

½ cup dried onion
¼ cup dried bell pepper

Seasonings:

1 tsp. garlic flakes
2 tsp. Italian seasoning
salt & pepper

Directions:

Combine all ingredients except cheese and heat through. Add Parmesan cheese and stir until melted in.

FOR EVERYDAY MEALS: Replace dried vegetables with double the amount of fresh. Drain beans.

Pumpkin Soup

SERVES 6

Cans/Jars:
1 (14-oz.) can vegetable broth
1 (29-oz.) can pumpkin puree
1 (14-oz.) can chicken broth

Dried:
2/3 cup powdered milk
2 Tbsp. dried bell pepper
¼ cup dried onion

Seasonings:
1/8 tsp. thyme
¼ tsp. nutmeg
½ tsp. salt
1–2 Tbsp. parsley flakes

Directions:

Dissolve powdered milk in broth in pan. Add all other ingredients except parsley. Heat through. Sprinkle parsley over each serving.

FOR EVERYDAY MEALS: Replace dried vegetables with double the amount of fresh. Replace powdered milk with 1 cup fresh.

Tuscan Supper

Cans/Jars:

1 (15-oz.) can green beans
1 (15-oz.) can great northern beans
1 (6-oz.) can mushrooms
1 (15-oz.) can diced tomatoes
1 (10-oz.) can cream of mushroom soup
1 (14-oz.) can vegetable broth
¼ cup Parmesan cheese

Dried:

1/3 cup dried onion

Seasonings:

1 Tbsp. Italian seasoning

Grain/Pasta:

½ cup corkscrew pasta

Directions:

Do not drain cans. Combine all ingredients except cheese. Simmer until pasta is done, stirring occasionally. Sprinkle Parmesan on each serving.

FOR EVERYDAY MEALS: Replace dried onion with 2/3 cup fresh.

Vegetable Cheese Soup

SERVES 8

Cans/Jars:

2 (15-oz.) cans creamed corn

1 (15-oz.) can diced potatoes

1 (15-oz.) can diced carrots

2 (14-oz.) cans chicken broth

1 (16-oz.) jar processed cheese

Seasonings:

3 Tbsp. onion flakes

½ tsp. pepper

1 tsp. celery seed, optional

Directions:

Do not drain cans. Combine all ingredients except cheese, and heat. Stir in cheese and heat through.

Veggie Stew

SERVES 10

Cans/Jars:

2 (15-oz.) cans diced potatoes
1 (15-oz.) can carrots
2 (15-oz.) cans diced tomatoes
1 (15-oz.) can green beans
1 (15-oz.) can corn
1 (15-oz.) can butter beans
4 (12-oz.) cans V-8 juice
2 (14-oz.) cans chicken broth

Dried:

½ cup dried onion
¼ cup dried celery

Seasonings:

1½ tsp. thyme
1 Tbsp. parsley flakes

Grain/Pasta:

½ cup rice

Directions:

Do not drain cans. Mix all ingredients together and simmer until rice is tender. Run a wand blender through it to partially puree and thicken.

FOR EVERYDAY MEALS: Replace dried vegetables with double the amount of fresh.

Wild Rice Casserole

SERVES 4-6

Cans/Jars:

1 (15-oz.) can stewed tomatoes
1 (2.5-oz.) can sliced olives, undrained
1 (6-oz.) can mushrooms, undrained
1 (8-oz.) can tomato sauce
1 (8-oz.) block processed cheese, cubed
1 (14-oz.) can vegetable broth

Grain/Pasta:

Small box wild rice (approximately ⅔ cup)

Dried:

½ cup dried onion

Directions:

Combine all ingredients in a casserole dish. Cover and bake at 250° for 3 hours. Or cook in crock pot 4–5 hours on low. Remove cover last 15 minutes of cooking time.

FOR EVERYDAY MEALS: Replace dried onion with 1 cup fresh.

Beef

All-in-one Casserole

Cans/Jars:
1 (10- to 15-oz.) can beef
1 (15-oz.) can corn
1 (6-oz.) can mushrooms
1 (16-oz.) jar salsa
1 (8-oz.) jar processed cheese
2 (15-oz.) cans diced tomatoes
1 (14-oz.) can beef broth

Grain/Pasta:
5 cups noodles

Dried:
½ cup dried onion
½ cup dried bell pepper

Seasonings:
salt & pepper

Directions:

Combine all ingredients in crock pot except noodles, tomatoes, and broth. Stir together gently. Place noodles on top, then tomatoes, and then broth. Cook on low for 4 hours.

FOR EVERYDAY MEALS: Replace dried vegetables with double the amount of fresh.

BBQ Beef Stew

SERVES 4-6

Cans/Jars:

1 (10- to 15-oz.) can beef
1 (15-oz.) can potatoes, drained
1 (15-oz.) can carrots, drained
1 (16-oz.) jar whole onions, drained
1 (16-oz.) bottle BBQ sauce

Dried:

2 Tbsp. dried celery, optional

Seasonings:

salt & pepper

Directions:

Combine all ingredients in large pot and heat through.

For everyday meals: Replace dried celery with 2 ribs celery, sliced.

Bean Bake

SERVES 6

Cans/Jars:
1 (10- to 15-oz.) can beef
3 Tbsp. bacon crumbles
1 (15-oz.) can lima beans
1 (15-oz.) can pork & beans
1 (15-oz.) can kidney beans
1 cup BBQ sauce

Directions:

Do not drain cans. Combine all ingredients and heat through. I recommend cooking this slowly in a crock pot so the flavors have time to meld.

Beef Barley Stew

SERVES 6

Cans/Jars:
1 (10- to 15-oz.) can beef
1 (15-oz.) can carrots
1 (6-oz.) can mushrooms
3 (14-oz.) cans beef broth

Dried:
½ cup dried onion
¼ cup dried bell pepper

Seasonings:
½ tsp. thyme
½ tsp. basil
½ tsp. garlic powder
salt & pepper
1 bay leaf

Grain/Pasta:
¾ cup barley

Directions:

Do not drain cans. Mix all ingredients together in pot. Cook until barley is tender (about 1 hour simmering on stove top or 3 hours on high in crock pot). Remove bay leaf before serving.

FOR EVERYDAY MEALS: Replace dried vegetables with double the amount of fresh.

Beef Minestrone

SERVES 10

Cans/Jars:
1 (10- to 15-oz.) can beef
2 (15-oz.) cans Italian-style tomatoes
1 (15-oz.) can garbanzo beans
1 (15-oz.) can green beans
1 (15-oz.) can zucchini in tomato
1 (14-oz.) can beef broth

Dried:
½ cup dried onion

Seasonings:
2 Tbsp. Italian seasoning
1 Tbsp. parsley flakes

Grain/Pasta:
1 cup small macaroni

Directions:

Do not drain cans. Combine all ingredients in a large pot and simmer until macaroni is done, stirring occasionally. In a crock pot, heat on low for 3 hours.

Note: Overcooking will make the macaroni too soft.

FOR EVERYDAY MEALS: Replace dried onion with 1 cup fresh, sauté in a little oil.

Beef Noodle Casserole

SERVES 6-8

Cans/Jars:

1 (10- to 15-oz.) can beef
1 (15-oz.) can corn
1 (6-oz.) can mushrooms
1 (16-oz.) jar salsa
2 (15-oz.) cans diced tomatoes
1 (8-oz.) block processed cheese, cubed

Dried:

½ cup dried onions
½ cup dried bell pepper

Seasonings:

salt & pepper

Grain/Pasta:

6-8 oz. noodles

Directions:

Do not drain cans. Mix all ingredients together except cheese, and simmer until noodles are tender, stirring frequently. Add cheese and stir until cheese melts. (Or, reserve half of cheese, turn mixture into casserole dish, top with reserved cheese and bake at 350° for 15–20 minutes.)

FOR EVERYDAY MEALS: Replace dried vegetables with double the amount of fresh.

Beef Stew Ole

SERVES 6

Cans/Jars:
1 (10- to 15-oz.) can beef, undrained
1 (15-oz.) can carrots, undrained
1 (15-oz.) can diced potatoes, undrained
1 (8-oz.) can tomato sauce
2 (14-oz.) cans beef broth

Seasonings:
2-3 Tbsp. taco seasoning
salt & pepper

Grain/Pasta:
1 cup rice

Directions:

Combine all ingredients except rice. Bring to a boil. Add rice, cover, reduce heat, and simmer until rice is done.

Beefy Soup

SERVES 6-8

Cans/Jars:
1 (10- to 15-oz.) can beef
1 (15-oz.) can tomatoes
1 (15-oz.) can potatoes
1 (15-oz.) can carrots
1 (15-oz.) can corn or mixed corn and peas
1 (14-oz.) can beef broth
1 can beef gravy

Dried:
½ cup onion
¼ cup celery

Seasonings:
½ tsp basil
salt & pepper

Directions:

Do not drain cans; use all the juices. Combine all ingredients and heat through.

FOR EVERYDAY MEALS: Replace dried vegetables with double the amount of fresh.

Broccoli Beef Soup

SERVES 4-6

Cans/Jars:

1 (10- to 15-oz.) can beef, undrained

2 (14-oz.) cans beef broth

2 (12-oz.) cans V-8 juice

Dried:

1 cup dried broccoli

½ cup dried onions

Seasonings:

1 tsp. garlic flakes

1 tsp. basil

1 Tbsp. parsley flakes

1 bay leaf

Grain/Pasta:

8 oz. curly noodles

Directions:

Combine all ingredients and simmer until noodles are done, stirring frequently. Remove bay leaf before serving.

FOR EVERYDAY MEALS: Replace dried vegetables with double the amount of fresh.

Chili

Cans/Jars:
1 (10- to 15-oz.) can beef, undrained
1 (8-oz.) can tomato sauce
1 (15-oz.) can diced tomatoes
1 (4-oz.) can diced green chilies, undrained
1 (15-oz.) can pinto beans, undrained
1 (15-oz.) can kidney beans, undrained
1 (14-oz.) can chicken broth
½ cup ketchup, optional

Dried:
½ cup dried bell pepper

Seasonings:
1 Tbsp. onion flakes
1 tsp. garlic powder
2–3 Tbsp. chili seasoning
2 Tbsp. brown sugar
2 Tbsp. vinegar

Directions:
Combine all ingredients and heat through.

FOR EVERYDAY MEALS: Replace dried peppers with 1 cup fresh.

Chili Mole

Grain/Pasta:
8 oz. spaghetti

Cans/Jars:
1 (14-oz.) can beef broth
1 (10- to 15-oz.) can beef
2 (15-oz.) cans Mexican-style corn
1 (8-oz.) can tomato sauce
1 (15-oz.) can kidney beans

Dried:
½ cup dried onion

Seasonings:
2 Tbsp. garlic flakes
2 Tbsp. chili powder
1 Tbsp. unsweetened cocoa powder
½ tsp. cinnamon
¼ tsp. allspice

Directions:

Simmer spaghetti in broth until softened, stirring occasionally. Do not drain cans. Combine remaining ingredients in pot. Add undrained spaghetti. Heat through.

FOR EVERYDAY MEALS: Replace dried onion with 1 cup fresh. Omit broth and cook spaghetti separately. Serve mixture over spaghetti and garnish with more onion and grated cheese.

Chili Stew

SERVES 4-6

Cans/Jars:

1 (10- to 15-oz.) can beef
1 (15-oz.) can potatoes
2 (15-oz.) cans kidney beans
1 (15-oz.) can diced tomatoes
1 (15-oz.) can carrots
1 (14-oz.) can beef broth

Dried:

½ cup dried celery
1/3 cup dried onion

Seasonings:

½ tsp. chili powder
½ tsp. Worcestershire sauce

Grain/Pasta:

½ cup rice

Directions:

Do not drain cans. Combine all ingredients and simmer until rice is done, stirring occasionally.

FOR EVERYDAY MEALS: Replace dried vegetables with double the amount of fresh.

Chinese Dinner

SERVES 6

Cans/Jars:
1 (10- to 15-oz.) can beef, undrained
1 (10-oz.) can chicken noodle soup
1 (10-oz.) can cream of mushroom soup
1 (12-oz.) can Chop Suey vegetables, undrained

Dried:
½ cup dried onion
½ cup dried bell pepper
¼ cup dried celery

Seasonings:
1½ tsp. soy sauce

Grain/Pasta:
1 (5-oz.) can chow mein noodles*

Directions:
Combine all ingredients in pot except noodles; heat through. Serve over chow mein noodles (or rice).

For everyday meals:
Omit dried vegetables. Add fresh: 2 ribs sliced celery, 1 diced onion, 1 diced green pepper.

*Chow mein noodles are not labeled for 2 years' storage, so rotate them more often.

Chinese Pepper Beef

SERVES 4-6

Cans/Jars:

1 (15-oz.) can bean sprouts
1 (5-oz.) can water chestnuts
1 (14-oz.) can beef broth
1 (10- to 15-oz.) can beef
1 (15-oz.) can diced tomatoes
¼ cup slivered almonds,* for garnish, optional

Grain/Pasta:

1¼ cups rice

Dried:

⅔ cup dried bell pepper

Seasonings:

1 Tbsp. cornstarch
1 tsp. garlic powder
3 Tbsp. soy sauce
1 tsp. sugar
2 Tbsp. onion flakes

Directions:

Stir cornstarch into liquid drained from bean sprouts in a bowl and set aside. Cook rice in broth in separate pot. Add remaining ingredients to pot except rice and cornstarch mixture. Simmer 10 minutes. Stir in cornstarch mixture and simmer an additional 10 minutes or until sauce thickens. Serve over rice. Top each serving with almonds.

FOR EVERYDAY MEALS: Replace dried peppers with two whole fresh peppers, diced. Omit broth. Cook rice separately.

*Store nuts in fridge or freezer.

Coconutty Beef Curry

SERVES 4-6

Grain/Pasta:
1¼ cups rice

Cans/Jars:
1 (14-oz.) can beef broth
1 (13.5-oz.) can coconut milk
1 (10- to 15-oz.) can beef
1 (15-oz.) can diced potatoes, drained
1 (15-oz.) can carrots, drained
1 (15-oz.) can peas, drained

Seasonings:
2 Tbsp. flour
1 Tbsp. curry powder
¼ tsp. red pepper flakes, optional
1 envelope onion soup mix
2 Tbsp. dried cilantro (or parsley)
 for garnish

Directions:

Cook rice in broth in separate pot. Stir flour into coconut milk in pot. Add remaining ingredients except cilantro. Heat through, stirring occasionally, until flour cooks and thickens the juices a bit. Serve over rice. Garnish with cilantro.

Cook All Day Dinner

SERVES 6

Grain/Pasta:
1 box wild rice (approximately ⅔ cup)

Cans/Jars:
1 (10- to 15-oz.) can beef
1 (6-oz.) can mushrooms
1 (15-oz.) can carrots
2 (14-oz.) cans beef broth
1 (10-oz.) can beef gravy

Dried:
¼ cup dried celery
½ cup dried onion

Seasonings:
2 tsp. season salt

Directions:

In bottom of crock pot, layer rice, then dried vegetables and salt, then canned items, undrained. Cook on low 6-8 hours.

FOR EVERYDAY MEALS: Replace dried vegetables with double the amount of fresh. Add ½ cup slivered almonds.

Corny Chili

Cans/Jars:

1 (10- to 15-oz.) can beef
1 (15-oz.) can Italian-style diced tomatoes
1 (6-oz.) can tomato paste
1 (15-oz.) can corn
1 (15-oz.) can kidney beans

Dried:

¼ cup dried onion
¼ cup dried bell pepper

Seasonings:

¼ tsp. thyme
1 Tbsp. chili powder
salt & pepper

Directions:

Do not drain cans. Combine all ingredients together and heat through.

For EVERYDAY MEALS: Replace dried vegetables with double the amount of fresh.

Creamy Beef Soup

SERVES 6

Cans/Jars:
1 (15-oz.) can diced potatoes
1 (15-oz.) can mixed vegetables
1 (10- to 15-oz.) can beef
1 (12-oz.) can V-8 juice
1 (10-oz.) can cream of mushroom soup
1 (10-oz.) can cream of celery soup

Dried:
½ cup sour cream powder
½ cup dried onion

Seasonings:
salt & pepper

Directions:

Combine juice from potatoes and vegetables in pan. Whisk in sour cream powder, stirring until dissolved. Add remaining ingredients and heat through.

FOR EVERYDAY MEALS: Replace dried ingredients with 1 cup fresh onion and ½ cup fresh sour cream.

Creamy Beefy Casserole

SERVES 6

Cans/Jars:
1 (10- to 15-oz.) can beef
1 (10-oz.) can cream of mushroom soup
1 (15-oz.) can diced tomatoes
1 (14-oz.) can beef broth
1 (8-oz.) block processed cheese, cubed

Dried:
½ cup dried onion

Seasonings:
salt & pepper

Grain/Pasta:
1½ cups rice

Directions:

Combine all ingredients but cheese and rice. Bring to a boil. Add rice, reduce heat, cover, and simmer until rice is done. Add cheese and continue stirring until cheese melts. (Or reserve half of cheese, turn mixture into casserole dish, top with reserved cheese, and bake at 375° for 15–20 minutes.)

FOR EVERYDAY MEALS: Replace dried onion with 1 cup fresh.

Cuban Dinner

SERVES 6

Grain/Pasta:
1¼ cups rice

Cans/Jars:
1 (14-oz.) can beef broth
1 (10- to 15-oz.) can beef
2 (15-oz.) cans diced tomatoes
1 (4-oz.) can diced green chilies, undrained
1 (6-oz.) can tomato paste
1 (6-oz.) can cranberry juice (or apple)
¼ cup sliced green olives with pimiento

Dried:
½ cup dried onion
¼ cup raisins

Seasonings:
2 Tbsp. garlic flakes
2 tsp. oregano
salt & pepper

Directions:

Cook rice in broth. In a separate pot, combine all other ingredients except olives and heat through. Serve over rice. Garnish with olives.

FOR EVERYDAY MEALS: Replace dried onion with 1 cup fresh. Omit broth and cook rice in water.

Diner Soup

Cans/Jars:

1 (10- to 15-oz.) can beef
1 (10-oz.) can tomato soup
1 (8-oz.) can tomato sauce
1 (14-oz.) can beef broth
1 (15-oz.) can green beans, undrained

Grain/Pasta:

⅔ cup quick-cooking rice

Dried:

½ cup dried onion

Seasonings:

2 tsp. parsley flakes
⅛ tsp. pepper

Directions:

Combine all ingredients together except rice and bring to a boil. Stir in rice, cover, reduce heat, and simmer on low until rice is done.

FOR EVERYDAY MEALS: Replace dried onion with 1 cup fresh.

Dried Beef & Noodles

SERVES 6

Grain/Pasta:

8 oz. noodles

Cans/Jars:

1 (14-oz.) can vegetable broth
1 (11.5-oz.) jar dried beef
1 (10-oz.) can cream of mushroom soup
1 (6-oz.) can mushrooms, undrained
1 (12-oz.) can evaporated milk
1 (8-oz.) block processed cheese, cubed

Directions:

Simmer noodles in broth until softened, stirring occasionally. Tear beef into 1-inch pieces. Mix all ingredients together in pot. Heat through.

Note: This is quite salty, so you might want to rinse the beef. You also might want only 4 ounces of the cheese, so don't add it all at once.

German Dinner

Cans/Jars:

1 (14-oz.) can vegetable broth
1 (10- to 15-oz.) can beef
1 (32-oz.) can sauerkraut, undrained
2 (12-oz.) cans V-8 juice

Dried:

1½ cups dried potatoes (pearls or flakes)
½ cup dried bell pepper
¼ cup dried celery
½ cup dried spinach, optional

Directions:

Bring broth to a boil. Remove from heat and stir in dried potatoes. Combine remaining ingredients in a separate pot and heat through. Serve over potatoes.

FOR EVERYDAY MEALS: Omit dried vegetables. Add fresh: 1 small grated green pepper, ½ cup chopped celery, 1 package frozen chopped spinach, thawed and squeezed dry. Omit broth and prepare potatoes (fresh or dried) using water.

Granny Made Plenty

SERVES 10-12

Cans/Jars:
2 (10- to 15-oz.) cans beef
1 (24- to 30-oz.) jar spaghetti sauce
1 (15-oz.) can corn
2 (14-oz.) cans beef broth
1 (8-oz.) block processed cheese, cubed

Grain/Pasta:
8 oz. macaroni

Dried:
½ cup dried onion

Seasonings:
2 tsp. chili powder
2 tsp. garlic powder
2 Tbsp. brown sugar
salt & pepper

Directions:

Combine all ingredients except cheese in pot. Simmer until macaroni is done, stirring occasionally. Add cheese to mixture, stirring gently until it melts in.

FOR EVERYDAY MEALS: Replace dried onion with 1 cup fresh.

Green Beans & Beef

Grain/Pasta:

1¼ cups brown rice

Cans/Jars:

1 (14-oz.) can beef broth
1 (10- to 15-oz.) can beef
2 (15-oz.) cans green beans, drained
1 (15-oz.) jar Mexican-style cheese (queso)*

Directions:

Cook rice in broth in a large pot. Add beef and beans and bring to a simmer. Stir in cheese and heat through.

 *Queso can be spicy. Add a little at a time and taste, so it doesn't get too hot for you.

Hodgepodge

SERVES 6

Cans/Jars:

1 (10- to 15-oz.) can beef
2 (10-oz.) cans minestrone soup
1 (15-oz.) can baked beans
1 (14-oz.) can beef broth

Dried:

⅓ cup dried onion

Seasonings:

1 Tbsp. Worcestershire sauce

Directions:

Combine all ingredients and heat through.

FOR EVERYDAY MEALS: Replace dried onion with ⅔ cup fresh.

Jackpot Pie

Cans/Jars:
1 (10- to 15-oz.) can beef
1 (15-oz.) can creamed corn
1 (10-oz.) can tomato soup
1 (14-oz.) can beef broth
1 (8-oz.) jar processed cheese

Grain/Pasta:
6 oz. crinkly noodles

Dried:
¼ cup dried onion

Seasonings:
1 Tbsp. Worcestershire sauce
1 tsp. sage
½ tsp. chili powder, optional
salt & pepper

Directions:

Combine all ingredients except cheese and simmer until noodles are tender, stirring occasionally. Put a dollop of cheese on each serving.

FOR EVERYDAY MEALS: Replace dried onion with ½ cup fresh.

Lena's Goulash

SERVES 4-6

Grain/Pasta:

1½ cups macaroni

Cans/Jars:

1 (14-oz.) can beef broth
1 (10- to 15-oz.) can beef
2 (15-oz.) cans diced tomatoes

Dried:

¼ cup dried onion

Seasonings:

1 Tbsp. garlic flakes
salt & pepper

Directions:

In large pot, simmer macaroni in broth until softened. Add remaining ingredients and heat through.

FOR EVERYDAY MEALS: Replace dried onion with ½ cup fresh. Omit broth. Cook macaroni separately.

Macaroni Beef

Grain/Pasta:
1 cup macaroni

Cans/Jars:
1 (14-oz.) can beef broth
1 (10- to 15-oz.) can beef
1 (15-oz.) can corn, undrained
1 (8-oz.) can tomato sauce

Dried:
⅓ cup dried onion

Seasonings:
1 Tbsp. brown sugar
¼ tsp. chili powder
salt & pepper

Directions:

Simmer macaroni in broth until softened. Add remaining ingredients and heat through.

For EVERYDAY MEALS: Replace dried onion with ⅔ cup fresh. Omit broth and cook macaroni in water.

Many-veggie Beef Stew

SERVES 12-15

Cans/Jars:

2 (10- to 15-oz.) cans beef
1 (15-oz.) can green beans
1 (15-oz.) can corn
1 (15-oz.) can peas
2 (15-oz.) cans carrots
2 (15-oz.) cans diced potatoes
1 (10-oz.) can tomato soup
1 (10-oz.) can cream of celery soup
1 (10-oz.) can cream of mushroom soup

Dried:

½ cup dried onion
½ cup dried bell pepper
¼ cup dried celery

Seasonings:

1 Tbsp. Worcestershire sauce
1 tsp. garlic powder
salt & pepper

Directions:

Do not drain cans. Mix all ingredients together in pot and heat through.

FOR EVERYDAY MEALS: Replace dried vegetables with fresh, doubling the amounts.

Mexican Goulash

SERVES 10-12

Cans/Jars:
1 (10- to 15-oz.) can beef
2 (15-oz.) cans diced tomatoes
1 (6-oz.) can tomato paste
1 (2.5-oz.) can sliced olives
1 (11-oz.) can Mexican-style corn
1 (15-oz.) can green beans
1 (15-oz.) can kidney beans
1 (4-oz.) can diced green chilies
1 (15-oz.) jar Mexican-style cheese (queso)*

Dried:
1 cup dried onion
½ cup dried bell pepper

Seasonings:
1 Tbsp. taco seasoning
salt & pepper
Dash hot pepper sauce, optional

Directions:

Do not drain cans. Combine all ingredients except cheese in large pot. Simmer until vegetables are done. Put a dollop of cheese on each serving.

FOR EVERYDAY MEALS: Replace dried vegetables with double the amount of fresh. Drain beans and corn.

*Queso can be spicy. Look for hot, medium, or mild.

Mushroom Noodle Soup

SERVES 4-6

Cans/Jars:
1 (10- to 15-oz.) can beef
2 (14-oz.) cans beef broth
2 (6-oz.) cans mushrooms

Grain/Pasta:
3 oz. noodles

Dried:
¼ cup dried onion

Seasonings:
½ tsp. garlic flakes
1 tsp. parsley flakes
salt & pepper

Directions:

Do not drain cans. Combine all ingredients and simmer until noodles are done, stirring frequently.

For everyday meals: Replace dried onion with ½ cup fresh.

Nancy's Beef & Sour Cream

SERVES 4-6

Cans/Jars:
1 (14-oz.) can beef broth
1 (10- to 15-oz.) can beef
1 (15-oz.) can diced tomatoes
1 (12-oz.) can V-8 juice

Grain/Pasta:
8 oz. noodles (3 cups)

Dried:
1 cup sour cream powder
½ cup dried onion

Seasonings:
2 tsp. celery salt
2 tsp. Worcestershire sauce

Directions:

Dissolve sour cream powder in ¼ cup broth. Set aside. Combine all other ingredients. Simmer, covered, until noodles are done, stirring frequently. Stir in sour cream mixture and heat through.

FOR EVERYDAY MEALS: Replace dried onion with 1 cup fresh. Replace sour cream powder with 1 cup fresh.

Party Beans

SERVES 12

Cans/Jars:
1 (10- to 15-oz.) can beef
2.5 oz. bacon crumbles
2 (15-oz.) cans green beans, drained
2 (15-oz.) cans butter beans, drained
2 (15-oz.) cans kidney beans, drained and rinsed
2 (15-oz.) cans baked beans
1 (16-oz.) bottle barbecue sauce

Dried:
½ cup dried onion
¼ cup dried bell pepper

Seasonings:
¼ cup brown sugar

Directions:

Combine all ingredients and heat through. Good in a crock pot.

FOR EVERYDAY MEALS: Replace dried vegetables with double the amount of fresh.

Patchwork Hash

SERVES 6

Cans/Jars:

1 (10- to 15-oz.) can beef
1 (15-oz.) can corn
1 (15-oz.) can kidney beans, drained
1 (15-oz.) can diced tomatoes
1 (14-oz.) can beef broth
1 (8-oz.) jar processed cheese

Grain/Pasta:

1¼ cups rice

Dried:

¼ cup dried onion

Directions:

Cook rice in broth in separate pot. Combine beef, corn, beans, tomatoes, and onions in pot. Do not drain cans. Heat through. Serve over rice with a dollop of cheese on top of each serving.

FOR EVERYDAY MEALS: Use ½ cup fresh onion in place of dry. Omit broth and cook rice in water.

109

Santa Rosa Cheese Soup

SERVES 6-8

Cans/Jars:

1 (10- to 15-oz.) can beef
1 (15-oz.) can corn
1 (15-oz.) can kidney beans
1 (15-oz.) can diced tomatoes with green chilies
1 (15-oz.) can stewed tomatoes
1 (16-oz.) block processed cheese, cubed

Seasonings:

2 Tbsp. taco seasoning

Directions:

Do not drain cans. Combine all in pot except cheese.
Bring to a simmer and add cheese, stirring until cheese
melts in.

Scalloped Potatoes Santa Fe

SERVES 4-6

Cans/Jars:
1 (10- to 15-oz.) can beef
1 (15-oz.) can potatoes
1 (15-oz.) can corn
1 (15-oz.) can Mexican-style tomatoes
1 (8-oz.) block processed cheese, cubed

Dried:
¼ cup dried onion

Seasonings:
2 tsp. parsley flakes
1 tsp. taco seasoning

Directions:

Do not drain cans; use all the juices. Mix all ingredients together and heat through.

FOR EVERYDAY MEALS: Replace dried onion with ½ cup fresh.

111

Simply Stew

SERVES 4

Cans/Jars:

1 (10- to 15-oz.) can beef
2 (15-oz.) cans diced potatoes
1 (15-oz.) can carrots
1 (8-oz.) can tomato sauce
1 (14-oz.) can beef broth

Seasonings:

½ envelope onion soup mix

Directions:

Do not drain cans. Mix all ingredients together in pot and
heat through.

Sorta Stroganoff

Cans/Jars:
1 (10- to 15-oz.) can beef
1 (6-oz.) can mushrooms, undrained
1 (10-oz.) can cream of mushroom soup
1 oz. bacon crumbles
1 (12-oz.) can evaporated milk

Grain/Pasta:
1 cup quick-cooking rice

Dried:
½ cup sour cream powder
¼ cup dried onion
¼ cup dried celery

Seasonings:
salt & pepper
1 tsp. garlic powder
½ tsp. paprika
2 tsp. Worcestershire sauce

Directions:

Whisk sour cream powder into milk in pot. Add all ingredients except rice. Bring to a boil. Stir in rice, cover, reduce heat, and simmer until rice is done. Fluff with a fork.

FOR EVERYDAY MEALS: Replace dried vegetables with double the amount of fresh.

Spaghetti Casserole

SERVES 10

Cans/Jars:
1 (10- to 15-oz.) can beef
1 (10-oz.) can cream of mushroom soup
1 (24- to 30-oz.) jar spaghetti sauce with vegetables
1 (6-oz.) can mushrooms, drained
1 (8-oz.) jar processed cheese
¼ cup Parmesan cheese
1 (14-oz.) can beef broth

Grain/Pasta:
8 oz. spaghetti, broken in 2-inch pieces

Dried:
¼ cup dried onion

Seasonings:
1 Tbsp. garlic flakes
2 Tbsp. Parmesan cheese

Directions:

Simmer spaghetti in broth until softened, stirring occasionally. Do not drain. Combine all ingredients except Parmesan cheese. Spread in sprayed 8x12 casserole dish and top with Parmesan. Bake at 400° for 20–25 minutes.

FOR EVERYDAY MEALS: Replace dried onion with ½ cup fresh. Omit broth and cook spaghetti before mixing with other ingredients.

Spanish Rice

Cans/Jars:

1 (10- to 15-oz.) can beef
2 (15-oz.) cans Mexican-style tomatoes
1 (8-oz.) can tomato sauce
1 (14-oz.) can beef broth

Grain/Pasta:

1¼ cups rice, regular or quick cooking

Dried:

½ cup dried onion
½ cup dried bell pepper

Seasonings:

2 tsp. chili powder
2 tsp. Worcestershire sauce
salt & pepper

Directions:

Combine all except rice. Bring to a boil. Stir in rice, reduce heat, cover, and simmer until rice is done. Fluff with a fork.

FOR EVERYDAY MEALS: Replace dried vegetables with fresh, 1 cup each.

Supper-in-a-dish

SERVES 8

Cans/Jars:

1 (10- to 15-oz.) can beef
1 (15-oz.) can sliced potatoes
1 (15-oz.) can carrots
1 (15-oz.) can peas
1 (10-oz.) can cream of mushroom soup
1 (8-oz.) jar processed cheese

Dried:

¼ cup dried onion
¼ cup dried celery
¼ cup dried bell pepper

Seasonings:

salt & pepper

Directions:

Drain juices from vegetables into pot. Stir in dried vegetables and let them sit a minute or two to rehydrate. Add other ingredients, except cheese. Heat through, stirring occasionally. Spread cheese on top and continue heating until cheese melts a bit.

FOR EVERYDAY MEALS: Replace dried vegetables with double the amount of fresh.

Suzi's Taco Soup

SERVES 8

Cans/Jars:
1 (10- to 15-oz.) can beef
1 (15-oz.) can hominy
1 (15-oz.) can kidney beans
1 (15-oz.) can corn
1 (15-oz.) can spicy Mexican-style tomatoes
2 (14-oz.) cans beef broth
1 (4-oz.) can diced green chilies

Grain/Pasta:
½ cup rice

Dried:
¼ cup dried onion

Seasonings:
2 Tbsp. taco seasoning
2 Tbsp. ranch dressing mix

Directions:

Do not drain cans. Combine all and simmer until rice is done.

FOR EVERYDAY MEALS: Replace dried onion with double the amount of fresh.

Tisha's Shepherd's Pie

SERVES 6

Cans/Jars:
1 (10- to 15-oz.) can beef
2 (15-oz.) cans green beans, drained
1 (15-oz.) can corn, drained
1 (10-oz.) can tomato soup (bisque style is great)
1 (14-oz.) can beef broth
1 (8-oz.) jar processed cheese

Dried:
¾ cup instant potatoes

Seasonings:
2 Tbsp. onion flakes
1 Tbsp. garlic flakes

Directions:
Bring broth to a boil, remove from heat, and stir in potatoes. Using about half the jar, drop cheese by spoonfuls into potatoes and stir gently. Set aside. In 9x13 casserole dish, mix beef, beans, corn, and soup. Spread potato mixture over top. Dot the top with small dollops of the remaining cheese. Bake at 400°, 15–20 minutes.

Tomato Chili Stew

SERVES 4

Cans/Jars:

1 (10-oz.) can bean with bacon soup

1 (10-oz.) can tomato soup

1 (15-oz.) can chili con carne (no beans)

1 (14-oz.) can beef broth

Dried:

¼ cup dried bell pepper

Directions:

Combine all ingredients and heat through.

Trucker Beans

SERVES 8

Cans/Jars:

1 (10- to 15-oz.) can beef
1 (12-oz.) can smoky-flavored Spam
1 (31-oz.) can pork & beans
1 (15-oz.) can light kidney beans
1 (15-oz.) can dark kidney beans
1 (15-oz.) can wax beans
1 (15-oz.) can lima beans

Seasonings:

1 cup ketchup
1 cup brown sugar
1 Tbsp. spicy mustard

Directions:

Do not drain cans. Cube Spam and brown. Drain off fat. Combine with remaining ingredients and heat through.

Vegetable Noodle Soup

Cans/Jars:

1 (10- to 15-oz.) can beef, undrained
2 (15-oz.) cans mixed vegetables, undrained
2 (14-oz.) cans beef broth
2 (12-oz.) cans V-8 juice

Grain/Pasta:

½ cup small noodles

Dried:

½ cup dried onion

Seasonings:

½ tsp. celery salt
½ tsp. sugar
salt & pepper

Directions:

Combine all ingredients and simmer until noodles are done, stirring frequently.

FOR EVERYDAY MEALS: Replace dried onion with 1 cup fresh.

Fish

Clam Chowder

Cans/Jars:

2 (10-oz.) cans New England–style clam chowder
1 (10-oz.) can cream of celery soup
1 (10-oz.) can cream of potato soup
2 (12-oz.) cans evaporated milk

Dried:

¼ cup dried bell pepper

Directions:

Combine all ingredients and heat slowly, stirring occasionally.

FOR EVERYDAY MEALS: Omit dried peppers and garnish
each serving with finely chopped fresh peppers.

Crab Bisque

SERVES 4

Cans/Jars:
1 (6-oz.) can crab, with juices
1 (10-oz.) can cream of mushroom soup
1 (10-oz.) can cream of asparagus soup
2 (12-oz.) cans evaporated milk

Seasonings:
½ tsp. Worcestershire sauce

Directions:
Combine all ingredients and heat through.

Crabmeat Soup

Dried:

½ cup sour cream powder

Cans/Jars:

1 (14-oz.) can vegetable broth
1 (6-oz.) can crabmeat, with juice
1 (10-oz.) can tomato soup
1 (10-oz.) can split pea soup (yes, with bacon and ham)
1 (12-oz.) can evaporated milk

Directions:

Dissolve sour cream powder in broth in pan. Add remaining ingredients and heat through.

FOR EVERYDAY MEALS: Replace sour cream powder with ½ cup sour cream.

Crab with Wild Rice

SERVES 6

Can/Jars:

1 (6-oz.) can crab, with juices
1 (6-oz.) can mushrooms, undrained
1 (12-oz.) can evaporated milk
1 (5-oz.) can water chestnuts, undrained
1 (14-oz.) can vegetable broth

Grain/Pasta:

1 box wild rice (approximately ⅔ cup)

Seasonings:

1 Tbsp. onion flakes
3 bay leaves

Directions:

Mix all ingredients and heat slowly, stirring occasionally for 2 hours (4 hours in crock pot) or until rice is tender. Remove bay leaves before serving.

Creamy Salmon Chowder

Cans/Jars:
2 (14-oz.) cans chicken broth
2 (5-oz.) cans salmon, undrained
1 (15-oz.) can corn, undrained

Grain/Pasta:
¾ cup whole wheat berries

Dried:
½ cup sour cream powder
½ cup dried celery
½ cup dried onion

Seasonings:
1 Tbsp. dill weed

Directions:

In a medium pot, whisk sour cream powder into chicken broth. Add remaining ingredients. Simmer on low until wheat is tender (4 hours on stovetop or 8 hours in crock pot).

FOR EVERYDAY MEALS: Replace dried vegetables with double the amount of fresh. Replace dried sour cream with ½ cup fresh.

Creamy Tuna Veggie Skillet

SERVES 6-8

Cans/Jars:

1 (5- to 7-oz.) can tuna
1 (10-oz.) can cream of celery soup
1 (15-oz.) can carrots
1 (15-oz.) can green beans
1 (6-oz.) can mushrooms
1 (14-oz.) can chicken broth
1 (8-oz.) jar processed cheese
¼ cup Parmesan cheese

Grain/Pasta:

8 oz. corkscrew pasta

Seasonings:

1 Tbsp. onion flakes
1 tsp. parsley flakes
salt & pepper

Directions:

Do not drain cans. Combine all ingredients except cheeses. Simmer until pasta is done, stirring occasionally. Add cheeses, stirring until melted.

Italian Tuna

Grain/Pasta:
6 oz. noodles

Cans/Jars:
1 (14-oz.) can vegetable broth
1 (5- to 7-oz.) can tuna
1 (10-oz.) can cream of mushroom soup
1 (12-oz.) can evaporated milk
1 (6-oz.) can mushrooms, drained
1 (2.5-oz.) can sliced olives, drained
½ cup Parmesan cheese, divided

Dried:
¼ cup dried onion

Seasonings:
2 tsp. lemon juice
2 Tbsp. parsley flakes, for garnish

Directions:

Simmer noodles in broth until softened. Combine remaining ingredients except ¼ cup Parmesan cheese. Stir in undrained noodles. Spread in 8x12 casserole dish. Top with ¼ cup Parmesan and parsley. Bake at 375° for 20–25 minutes.

FOR EVERYDAY MEALS: Replace dried onion with ½ cup fresh. Omit broth. Cook noodles in water and drain.

Quickie Clam Chowder

SERVES 4

Cans/Jars:
1 (6.5-oz.) minced clams with juice
1 (15-oz.) can corn, undrained
2 (10-oz.) cans cream of potato soup

Seasonings:
1 tsp. onion flakes
½ tsp. garlic powder, optional

Directions:
Mix together all ingredients and heat through.

Salmon Noodle Casserole

SERVES 4

Grain/Pasta:
6 oz. noodles

Cans/Jars:
1 (14-oz.) can vegetable broth
1–2 (6-oz.) cans salmon with juice
1 (6-oz.) can mushrooms, drained
1 (15-oz.) can green beans, drained
1 (10-oz.) can cream of mushroom soup

Seasonings:
1 tsp. onion flakes
1 tsp. parsley flakes
1 tsp. dill weed
⅛ tsp. pepper

Directions:

Simmer noodles in broth until softened. Drain, reserving liquid. Add all other ingredients and stir together. If mixture is too thick, add in liquid from noodles. Spread mixture in a sprayed 8x8 baking dish. Bake at 350° for 25 minutes.

FOR EVERYDAY MEALS: Omit broth. Cook noodles in water.

Shrimp Alfredo

SERVES 4

Grain/Pasta:
6 oz. spaghetti, broken

Cans/Jars:
1 (14-oz.) can vegetable broth
2 (4-oz.) cans shrimp, drained
1 (15-oz.) can diced tomatoes
1 (24- to 30-oz.) jar Alfredo sauce
¼ cup Parmesan cheese, for garnish

Dried:
⅓ cup dried onion

Seasonings:
1 Tbsp. garlic flakes
1 Tbsp. basil

Directions:

Simmer spaghetti in broth until softened, stirring occasionally. Add all other ingredients except shrimp and bring back to a simmer. Stir in shrimp. Top each serving with Parmesan.

FOR EVERYDAY MEALS: Omit broth. Cook spaghetti in water and drain. Replace dried onion with ⅔ cup fresh onion and sauté it in butter before adding it in. Combine ingredients to make sauce and serve over spaghetti.

Shrimp & Veggies

Cans/Jars:
2 (4-oz.) cans shrimp
1 (15-oz.) can diced potatoes
1 (15-oz.) can diced tomatoes
1 (6-oz.) can tomato juice

Dried:
½ cup dried onion
½ cup dried bell pepper

Seasonings:
½ tsp. garlic flakes
1 tsp. parsley flakes
¼ tsp. pepper

Directions:

Do not drain cans. Use all juices. Combine all ingredients and heat through.

FOR EVERYDAY MEALS: Replace dried vegetables with double the amount of fresh.

Tuna a la King

SERVES 6

Cans/Jars:
1 (5- to 7-oz.) can tuna, drained
1 (6-oz.) can mushrooms, drained
1 (15-oz.) can peas, drained
1 (12-oz.) can evaporated milk
1 (14-oz.) can vegetable broth

Grain/Pasta:
1 cup quick-cooking rice

Dried:
½ cup sour cream powder

Seasonings:
1 tsp. parsley flakes
salt & pepper

Directions:

In a medium pot, whisk sour cream powder into chicken broth. Add remaining ingredients except rice. Bring to a boil. Add rice and stir. Cover and leave on lowest heat for 10 minutes. Fluff with fork.

FOR EVERYDAY MEALS: Replace sour cream powder with ½ cup fresh.

Tuna Casserole

Grain/Pasta:
6 oz. noodles

Cans/Jars:
1 (5- to 7-oz.) can tuna
1 (14-oz.) can vegetable broth
1 (10-oz.) can cream of celery soup
1 (15-oz.) can peas, drained
1 (6-oz.) can mushrooms
1 (5-oz.) can water chestnuts

Dried:
¼ cup dried celery
¼ cup dried onion

Directions:
Simmer noodles in broth until softened, stirring occasionally. Drain off broth. Soak dried vegetables in juice from mushrooms and water chestnuts. Combine all ingredients and spread mixture in a sprayed 8x8 baking dish. Bake at 350° for 25 minutes.

FOR EVERYDAY MEALS: Omit broth. Cook noodles separately. Drain mushrooms and water chestnuts. Replace dried vegetables with double the amount of fresh. Sprinkle with something crunchy (slivered almonds or crushed potato chips) before baking.

Tuna Chowder

SERVES 4

Cans/Jars:
1 (5- to 7-oz.) can tuna, undrained
2 (10-oz.) cans cream of potato soup
1 (12-oz.) can evaporated milk
2 oz. bacon crumbles

Dried:
2 Tbsp. dried onion
1 Tbsp. dried bell pepper

Seasonings:
¼ tsp. paprika

Directions:

Combine all ingredients and heat through.

FOR EVERYDAY MEALS: Replace dried vegetables with double the amount of fresh.

Vegetable Salmon Chowder

SERVES 8

Cans/Jars:
2 (14-oz.) cans vegetable broth
1 (6-oz.) can salmon, undrained
1 (15-oz.) can diced potatoes, undrained

Dried:
1 cup powdered milk
½ cup dried celery
¼ cup dried onion
1 Tbsp. dried bell pepper
½ cup instant potatoes

Seasonings:
1 Tbsp. dried parsley flakes
1 tsp. garlic flakes
2 tsp. lemon juice

Directions:

In a pan, dissolve powdered milk in broth. Add other ingredients except salmon and instant potatoes. Bring to a simmer, stir in instant potatoes. Remove from heat and stir until potatoes dissolve. Gently stir in salmon and heat through.

FOR EVERYDAY MEALS: Replace dried vegetables with double the amount of fresh. Omit 1 can broth. Replace powdered milk with 1½ cups fresh.

Ham & Bacon

Bavarian Kraut

SERVES 4

Cans/Jars:
1 (15-oz.) can sauerkraut
1 (23-oz.) jar applesauce
2 oz. bacon crumbles

Dried:
¼ cup dried onion

Seasonings:
1 tsp. parsley flakes
½ tsp. caraway seeds
1 tsp. brown sugar
⅛ tsp. pepper

Directions:

Partially drain sauerkraut, leaving enough juice to hydrate onions. Combine all ingredients and heat through.

FOR EVERYDAY MEALS: Replace dried onion with ½ cup fresh. Drain sauerkraut completely and prepare as above.

Black Beans & Ham Soup

SERVES 4-6

Cans/Jars:
2 (15-oz.) cans black beans, undrained
1 (5-oz.) can ham
1 (14-oz.) can beef consommé

Dried:
½ cup dried onion
¼ cup dried celery

Seasonings:
2 bay leaves
1 Tbsp. garlic flakes
1 Tbsp. parsley flakes, for garnish

Directions:

Combine all ingredients and heat through. Remove bay leaves. Use wand blender to partially mash beans and thicken soup. Ladle into bowls and sprinkle with parsley.

FOR EVERYDAY MEALS: Replace dried vegetables with double the amount of fresh.

Corn Chowder

Cans/Jars:

2.5 oz. bacon crumbles

2 (15-oz.) cans diced potatoes

2 (15-oz.) cans corn

1 (15-oz.) can creamed corn

1 (14-oz.) can vegetable broth

Dried:

½ cup dried onion

Seasonings:

1 Tbsp. sugar

1½ tsp. Worcestershire sauce

1 tsp. season salt

¼ tsp. pepper

Directions:

Do not drain cans. Combine all ingredients and heat through.

For everyday meals: Replace dried onion with 1 cup fresh.

Creamed Carrots with Bacon

SERVES 4

Cans/Jars:
2 (15-oz.) cans carrots
1 (10-oz.) can cream of celery soup
2 oz. bacon crumbles

Dried:
½ cup sour cream powder
¼ cup dried onion

Seasonings:
1 tsp. parsley flakes
salt & pepper

Directions:

Drain carrots into pan and stir sour cream powder into liquid, mixing until powder dissolves. Add all other ingredients and heat through.

FOR EVERYDAY MEALS: Replace dried onion with ½ cup fresh. Replace sour cream powder with ½ cup fresh. Drain carrots.

Gypsy Mix-up

Grain/Pasta:
6 oz. noodles

Cans/Jars:
1 (14-oz.) can chicken broth
2 (5-oz.) cans ham
1 (10-oz.) can cream of mushroom soup
1 (6-oz.) can mushrooms, drained
1 (14-oz.) can sauerkraut
1 (2-oz.) jar pimientos, drained (optional)

Seasonings:
3 Tbsp. onion flakes
½ tsp. caraway
1 tsp. brown sugar

Directions:

Simmer noodles in broth until softened. Drain. Combine all ingredients and heat through.

FOR EVERYDAY MEALS: Omit broth and cook noodles separately.

Ham Celery Bake

SERVES 4-6

Grain/Pasta:
¾ cup rice

Cans/Jars:
2 (5-oz.) cans ham
1 (8-oz.) can tomato sauce
1 (10-oz.) can cream of celery soup
1 (10-oz.) can cheese soup
1 (14-oz.) can chicken broth

Dried:
¾ cup dried celery
¼ cup dried onion

Seasonings:
1 tsp. chili powder, optional
1 Tbsp. parsley flakes
salt & pepper

Directions:

Cook rice in broth in large pot. Do not drain. Add remaining ingredients and spread in sprayed 8x8 casserole dish. Bake at 375° for 20–25 minutes.

FOR EVERYDAY MEALS: Replace dried vegetables with double the amount of fresh. Sauté them in a little oil before combining with other ingredients. Omit broth. Cook 1 cup rice in 1½ cups water and do not drain.

Ham Chili

SERVES 10-12

Cans/Jars:
2 (5-oz.) cans ham
1 (8-oz.) can tomato sauce
1 (40-oz.) can tomato juice
1 (15-oz.) can kidney beans, undrained
1 (14-oz.) can chicken broth
1 (2.5-oz.) can sliced olives, drained
1 (8-oz.) jar processed cheese

Grain/Pasta:
1 cup quick-cooking rice

Dried:
½ cup dried onion
½ cup dried bell pepper

Seasonings:
1 Tbsp. chili seasoning

Directions:

Combine all ingredients except rice, olives, and cheese. Bring to a boil. Stir in rice, cover, and simmer on low for 10 minutes or until rice is done. Add olives and cheese, stirring until cheese is melted.

FOR EVERYDAY MEALS: Replace dried vegetables with double the amount of fresh.

Ham Corn Chowder

SERVES 6

Cans/Jars:

1–2 (5-oz.) cans ham

1 (15-oz.) can potatoes

1 (15-oz.) can creamed corn

1 (12-oz.) can evaporated milk

1 (10-oz.) can cream of mushroom soup

Dried:

¼ cup dried onion

Seasonings:

1 tsp. parsley flakes

¼ tsp. pepper

Directions:

Combine all ingredients and heat through.

FOR EVERYDAY MEALS: Replace dried onion with ½ cup fresh.

Hammy Mac & Cheese

Grain/Pasta:

1½ cups macaroni

Cans/Jars:

1 (14-oz.) can chicken broth
1 (15-oz.) can diced tomatoes
1–2 (5-oz.) cans ham
1 (10-oz.) can cream of mushroom soup
1 (8-oz.) block of processed cheese, cubed

Seasonings:

3 Tbsp. onion flakes

Directions:

Simmer macaroni with broth and tomatoes until macaroni is done, stirring occasionally. Add remaining ingredients and heat until cheese melts.

FOR EVERYDAY MEALS: Omit broth. Cook macaroni separately in water and drain.

Ham with Ranch

SERVES 4

Cans/Jars:

2 (5-oz.) cans ham
1 (15-oz.) can potatoes
1 (10-oz.) can cream of potato soup
1 (15-oz.) can green veggies (limas, peas, beans, asparagus)
½ jar Ranch dip (approximately ¾ cup)

Directions:

Drain potatoes and green veggies. Mix all ingredients together and heat through.

Ham Yam Yum

Cans/Jars:

1 (15-oz.) can pineapple chunks or tidbits
1 (40-oz.) can sweet potatoes
1–2 (5-oz.) cans ham

Seasonings:

¼ cup brown sugar
2 tsp. corn starch, optional

Directions:

Drain juices from pineapple and sweet potatoes into pot. Stir in cornstarch and heat, stirring until juices thicken (or omit corn starch and discard juices). Add remaining ingredients and heat through.

Hawaiian Supper

SERVES 4-6

Dried:
¼ cup dried onion
¼ cup dried bell pepper

Cans/Jars:
1 (14-oz.) can chicken broth
1 (12-oz.) can Spam
1 (15-oz.) can crushed pineapple
1 (10-oz.) can tomato soup

Grain/Pasta:
1 cup rice

Directions:

Stir dried vegetables into ⅓ cup broth. Cook rice in remaining broth in separate pan. Meanwhile, cube and brown Spam. Drain off fat. Combine all ingredients except rice and heat through. Serve over rice.

FOR EVERYDAY MEALS: Omit broth and cook rice in water. Replace dried vegetables with double the amount of fresh. Sauté vegetables as you brown the Spam.

Vienna Soup

SERVES 6

Cans/Jars:

1 (10-oz.) can cream of celery soup

1 (10-oz.) can cream of chicken soup

1 (10-oz.) can French onion soup

1 (12-oz.) can evaporated milk

1 (15-oz.) can corn, drained

1 (5-oz.) can Vienna sausages, sliced ¼ in. thick

Directions:

Combine all ingredients and heat through.

Zesty Hominy

SERVES 4

Cans/Jars:

1 (15-oz.) can kidney beans

1 (30-oz.) can hominy

1 (7-oz.) jar green salsa*

1 oz. bacon crumbles

Seasonings:

1 tsp. Worcestershire sauce

2 tsp. yellow mustard

Directions:

Combine all ingredients and heat through.

*Salsa can be spicy. Add as much as your family will enjoy.

Just for Fun

Aunt Shirley's Cookies

MAKES 3 DOZEN

Cans/Jars:

1 box spice cake mix

1 (15-oz.) can pumpkin puree

1 (11- or 12-oz.) bag chocolate chips

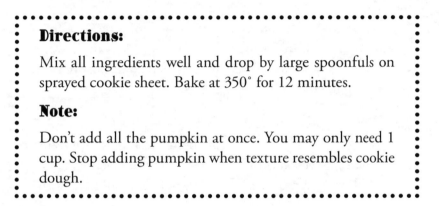

Directions:

Mix all ingredients well and drop by large spoonfuls on sprayed cookie sheet. Bake at 350° for 12 minutes.

Note:

Don't add all the pumpkin at once. You may only need 1 cup. Stop adding pumpkin when texture resembles cookie dough.

Soda Pop Cake

Cans/Jars:
1 box cake mix, any flavor
1 (12-oz.) can soda pop, any flavor

Directions:

Mix ingredients and microwave for 8 minutes in a 9x13 dish, covered and vented. Let stand for 10 minutes and turn onto a serving plate. You can also bake cake in oven using bake time on cake mix box.

Notes:

Using an electric mixer yields better results than mixing by hand. If you don't have 9x13 dish with a vented cover, use plastic wrap, pulled taut, and poke a small hole in the middle.

Ting-a-Lings

MAKES 2 DOZEN

Cans/Jars:

1 (11- or 12-oz.) bag baking chips, any flavor
1 (5-oz.) can chow mein noodles

Directions:

Melt baking chips in microwave (it takes approximately 2 minutes) and stir in noodles, mixing until noodles are evenly coated. Drop in cookie-size clumps on waxed paper and allow baking chips to harden.

Note:

This is a good way to use your stored chow mein noodles so that they do not go stale. Butterscotch chips are especially good.

Tips & Tricks

Vacation Easier

Vacationing in a time share condo is great, but have you ever gone shopping in an unfamiliar store and tried to plan meals with none of your usual "extras" on hand? I know I have wasted hours wandering the aisles trying to pull things together only to realize I would need to buy much larger sizes of some things than we could ever use up in a week. The recipes on this list do not require spices. They use only cans and simple extras, like onions and sour cream, which you can get fresh in any store. If you want to use fresh meat instead of canned, you can substitute a pound of hamburger, chicken tenders, or deli ham. You can also expand this list if you are willing to plan ahead and bring a few things from home. And, of course, most of these recipes would be great on a camp stove or done in a Dutch oven.

If you don't want to store seasonings, plan your 100-day storage from this list.

Vacation-Ready Recipes

CHICKEN

BBQ Chicken with Fruit
Chicken Broccoli Alfredo
Chicken Corn Chowder
Chicken Noodle Soup w/ Bacon
Chicken Taco Rice
    (use ½ pkg. taco seasoning)
Chicken Taco Soup
Mexican Chicken Casserole
Mulligan Stew
Quick Chicken
Scalloped Chicken & Corn
Tex-Mex Chicken & Rice
    (use 1 pkg. taco seasoning)

VEGGIES

Broccoli Cheese Soup
Mexican Tomato Corn Soup
    (use ½ pkg. taco seasoning)
Wild Rice Casserole

BEEF

All-in-one Casserole
BBQ Beef Stew
Bean Bake
Beef Noodle Casserole
Beef Stew Ole
    (use 1 pkg. taco seasoning)
Creamy Beef Soup
Creamy Beefy Casserole
Dried Beef & Noodles

German Dinner
Green Beans & Beef
Mexican Goulash
    (use ½ pkg. taco seasoning)
Patchwork Hash
Santa Rosa Cheese Soup
    (use 1 pkg. taco seasoning)
Simply Stew
Supper-in-a-dish
Suzi's Taco Soup
    (use 1 pkg. taco seasoning & 1
    pkg. ranch mix)
Tomato Chili Stew

FISH

Clam Chowder
Crabmeat Soup
Quickie Clam Chowder

HAM & BACON

Ham with Ranch
Ham Yam Yum
    (take ¼ cup brown sugar with
    you)
Hawaiian Supper
Vienna Soup

JUST FOR FUN

Aunt Shirley's Cookies
Soda Pop Cake
Ting-a-Lings

ORGANIZING

There are two basic approaches to organizing your pantry. You can store by the food type, with all the green beans together and all the mushroom soup together, or you can store by the meal, with all the makings for one type of meal together.

Whichever way you keep your main storage, I recommend that you have a handy spot on a shelf in your kitchen where you keep the ingredients for your next pantry meal. After your meal, move the ingredients for the next meal into position right away so there is always something you can put your hands on very quickly.

Tracking

You need a way to keep track of what ingredients you use, because you need to replenish your storage on a regular basis. You also need to check off each meal as you use it so that everything gets eaten. Without a way of keeping track, you could use up your family's favorites first and wind up needing to use the same recipe eight times in a row in order to keep the inventory balanced.

Keep two charts on your wall. One lists all the meals for which you have ingredients. The other is a list of all the things you want to keep in storage—your master inventory. Create these charts on your computer so that you can easily print out a fresh copy. Make modifications as you get to know what works best for you and your family. Your inventory can be a spreadsheet or just a simple list.

Here is a sample of what you would need to store to have the makings for 100 meals on hand. First, let's choose ten recipes.

1. Chicken & Beef Pot Luck
2. Chicken Taco Soup
3. Italian Chicken
4. Chili Stew
5. Many-veggie Beef Stew
6. Mexican Goulash
7. Patchwork Hash
8. Spaghetti Casserole
9. Black Bean & Ham Soup
10. Creamy Salmon Chowder

Now, let's assume you will be feeding six people. You will need to double the ingredients for the Taco Soup and the Salmon Chowder. The other recipes are sufficient for six or more. Then we multiply by ten, so you can make each recipe ten times.

DRIED

5 cups dried broccoli
22½ cups dried celery
   (2 #10 cans)
50 cups dried onion
   4 #10 cans
15 cups dried bell pepper
10 cups sour cream powder

MEAT & CHEESE

70 cans beef
40 cans chicken
10 cans ham
40 cans salmon
9 cups Parmesan cheese
20 (8-oz.) jars processed cheese
10 jars queso cheese

VEGETABLES

40 cans carrots
70 cans corn
10 cans Mexican corn
20 cans green beans
10 cans lima beans
20 cans mushrooms
10 cans peas
50 cans diced potatoes
10 cans sliced olives
50 cans diced tomatoes
20 cans Italian tomatoes
10 cans tomato paste
10 jars spaghetti sauce
30 cans green chilies
20 jars salsa

BEANS

20 cans black beans
40 cans kidney beans
20 cans ranch beans

SOUP

30 cans beef broth
10 cans beef consommé
70 cans chicken broth
10 cans cream of celery soup
20 cans cream of mushroom
soup
10 cans tomato soup

GRAIN

60 oz. pasta
30 cups rice
80 oz. spaghetti
15 cups whole wheat

SEASONINGS

20 bay leaves
4 Tbsp. chili powder
1¼ cups dill
1½ cups garlic flakes
4 Tbsp. garlic powder
Hot pepper sauce
4 Tbsp. Italian seasoning
4 Tbsp. mustard powder
4 cups parsley flakes
10 Tbsp. taco seasoning
8 oz. Worcestershire sauce
salt & pepper

When you pull things from storage, mark your inventory sheet. Every two or three weeks, take your inventory list to the store and buy replacements. When you stock your purchases, put up a new inventory sheet. There is no need to reserve these goods just for these recipes. If you want tomato soup for any reason, go ahead and grab it—just be sure to mark the chart. By having such a deep and varied supply on hand, you will find yourself saving time and money by not making so many trips to the store. (You may also become the go-to neighbor when someone needs to borrow a can of whatever.) As you develop your system, you will be able to watch for sales and case lot specials to keep everything stocked. Lots of canned foods come in cases of 12 or 24, so planning your meals by the dozen (8 recipes x 12 = 96 meals) would maximize the advantage of buying by the case.

Your other chart lists the names of your selected meals and the number of times each is to be used. This chart stays on the wall until you have rotated through everything (within two years). This chart could be a clipboard with a place for individual recipe cards. Each card would list the name of the dish, the number of times it is used in your plan, with room to check it off each time, and a list of ingredients. Or print copies of the recipe and put them in a pocket on the chart. Each time you prepare a meal, grab the recipe, gather the ingredients, and take the recipe to the kitchen. That copy of the recipe can then be discarded or returned to the back of its pocket and turned backwards so you can tell when you have used it enough times.

A third way to keep track—and the simplest—is to have one copy of each recipe and just turn it backward when you use it. Then, when all are facing backward, turn the recipes all over and start again. You don't have to keep track of how many times you've used it; you just need to be faithful in using one recipe each week. The chart is permanent, so you can get creative and make it pretty.

Don't become overwhelmed. Start simple. Just make a copy of each recipe after you have tested it and tape it on the wall. Make a check mark each time you use it. Add recipes as you continue your trial runs. After a while, you can graduate to whatever system you want to set up for long-term use.

Stashing

Allocating space in your home will require some adjustments. Be mindful of storage temperatures. Under the window in a non-insulated garage is not ideal. If you are fortunate enough to have basement storage, you just need appropriate shelving. There are commercial shelving systems available that make it easy to rotate your canned goods. For example, slanted shelves that let the cans roll into place for removal so you get the first-in-first-out effect, are ideal if you have the space and the money. These are available in sizes to fit kitchen or pantry shelves or as tall, stand-alone units. Simply stacking cases probably takes the least space, but you have to exercise discipline to rearrange your stacks and use the oldest first.

Personally, I use shallow shelves, just two cans deep, and store by recipe. I have lots of bookshelves in my home, and I store the makings for one meal behind each row of books. There are creative ways to stash. A stack of cases and a tablecloth make a pretty good night stand or end table. If you keep shoes on your closet floor, put two or three layers of cases down first, and your shoes will be easier to reach! The problem is not so much space as priorities. You CAN do it.

DRIED FOODS & SOURCES

As you select your recipes, you will see which of the dried foods you need. As I tested recipes, I kept running into the need for green peppers and celery. Some recipes need a little more richness to taste really good, and the sour cream powder helps a lot. I also used dried broccoli and dried spinach. If you simply hate canned meats, you might want to try freeze-dried meats. I chose to use processed cheese in the recipes, but dried cheese powder is available, and you can even get freeze-dried mozzarella and cheddar. Freeze-dried foods cost more and take more room but probably give better quality. I did my testing with regular dehydrated veggies and found the results perfectly acceptable. If you choose freeze-dried, you might need to adjust the measurements and use more. You can find all the vegetables (green beans, corn, zucchini, and so on) in dried form, but for this book I chose to indicate the dried ingredients only for those that are not readily available in cans. The same philosophy applies to my use of processed cheese. I chose items you can find in a grocery store over items you need to order. When you use the dried veggies, be sure to let the mixture simmer long enough for the veggies to rehydrate.

These dried foods come in #10 cans and cost $10 to $15 for the vegetables and $20 or more for the sour cream. I suggest that you fill smaller (10 to 20 ounce) containers with dried onions and peppers for your spice shelf—you'll be using them a lot. Empty plastic jars that once held nuts or rice are great for this. Smaller quantities of dried vegetables (size 2.5) are available from Walton Feed and North Bay Trading.

You might be able to find the dried items locally. Look for preparedness dealers in your area. Sometimes you can get dried food items at a restaurant supply house, but they often carry them packaged in waxed cardboard, like a milk carton, which are unfortunately not designed for long-term storage.

The websites listed below have a good variety of dried foods. Some also offer emergency stoves. It's always a good idea to have an alternative means of cooking in your storage plan. If you find yourself needing to conserve heating resources, you can omit the rice or pasta and just bring things to a simmer (or even eat at room temperature).

These recipes use more canned milk than powdered, but you can certainly substitute one for the other. I've been told by more than one mother that Country Cream powdered milk, available from Grandma's Country, has the best taste.

Here are some websites to get you started:
AugusonFarms.com
BePrepared.com
EmergencyEssentials.com
GrandmasCountryfoods.com
NorthBayTrading.com
WaltonFeed.com
ShelfReliance.com (for pantry shelving)

RECIPES FOR FOUR OR SIX

If your family is small, you will want to select recipes that do not make big batches.

SERVES FOUR (*indicates 4-6 servings):

CHICKEN
African Chicken*
Buffalo Wing Chicken Soup
Chicken Barley Soup
Chicken Broccoli Alfredo*
Chicken Capri*
Chicken Chow Mein
Chicken Fettuccini
Chicken Mushroom Stew*
Chicken Paprika*
Chicken Taco Rice
Chicken Taco Soup
Italian Chicken*
Mediterranean Chicken
Quick Chicken
Southern Chicken Curry
Tamale Chicken*

VEGGIES
Basil Tomato Soup
Carrot Curry Soup
Pasta Grande
Pizza Beans*
Wild Rice Casserole*

BEEF
BBQ Beef Stew*
Broccoli Beef Soup*
Chili Stew*
Chinese Pepper Beef*
Coconutty Beef Curry*
Corny Chili*
German Dinner*
Green Beans & Beef
Lena's Goulash
Macaroni Beef*

Mushroom Noodle Soup*
Nancy's Beef & Sour Cream*
Scalloped Potatoes Santa Fe*
Simply Stew
Sorta Stroganoff
Tomato Chili Stew

FISH
Crab Bisque
Creamy Salmon Chowder
Italian Tuna*
Quickie Clam Chowder
Salmon Noodle Casserole

Shrimp & Veggies
Tuna Casserole
Tuna Chowder

HAM & BACON
Bavarian Kraut
Black Bean and Ham Soup*
Creamed Carrots w/ Bacon
Ham Celery Bake
Ham w/ Ranch
Ham Yam Yum*
Hawaiian Supper*
Zesty Hominy

SERVES SIX (*indicates 6-8 servings)

CHICKEN
Asian Chicken Soup
BBQ Chicken w/ Fruit
Brunswick Stew
Cheesy Chicken & Beans
Cheesy Menudo
Chicken a la King
Chicken Artichoke Curry
Chicken Basil
Chicken Caravan
Chicken Cashew
Chicken Creole
Chicken Macaroni Stew
Chicken Noodle Soup,
   Traditional
Chicken Noodle Soup w/
   Bacon
Chicken Rice Stew
Chicken Veggie Bake
Jambalaya
Mulligan Stew

Pumpkin Chili*
Scalloped Chicken & Corn
Sweet & Sour Chicken*
White Bean Chicken Chili

VEGGIES
Black Bean Veggie Soup
Minestrone
Pumpkin Soup
Tuscan Supper

BEEF
Bean Bake
Beef Barley Stew
Beef Noodle Casserole*
Beef Stew Ole
Beefy Soup*
Chinese Dinner
Cook All Day Dinner
Creamy Beef Casserole
Creamy Beef Soup
Cuban Dinner

Diner Soup
Dried Beef & Noodles
Hodgepodge
Jackpot Pie
Patchwork Hash
Santa Rosa Cheese Soup*
Spanish Rice*
Tisha's Shepherd's Pie
Vegetable Noodle Soup
Clam Chowder

Crabmeat Soup
Crab w/ Wild Rice
Creamy Tuna Veggie Skillet*
Tuna a la King
Corn Chowder
Gypsy Mix-up*
Ham Corn Chowder
Hammy Mac & Cheese
Vienna Soup

About the Author

Jan was born and raised in Sacramento and attended schools there through junior college. She earned bachelor's and master's degrees in sociology in Utah. For the next ten years, she worked in the medical computer industry, conducting sales presentations and training seminars in hospitals throughout the country.

Ever since high school, Jan dreamed of writing, drawing, or singing but thought she had no talent. She finally realized that such things do not necessarily spring forth unbidden but can be discovered and developed. She considers herself a late bloomer. When in her thirties, she left the business world to raise her children, and she was able to do intermittent freelance work—writing, drawing, and singing. She sang for ten seasons with Utah Opera Company.

Jan loves to read, especially cookbooks. Widowed in 2004, Jan now lives in Idaho. She has a son in Utah and a daughter in California.